Identity

THEMES FOR THE 21ST CENTURY

Titles in this series

Identity

Conversations with
Benedetto Vecchi

ZYGMUNT BAUMAN

LEARNING RESOURCES
CENTRE

Havering College
of Further and Higher Education

polity

First published in 2004 by Polity Press.
Reprinted 2004, 2005, 2006

Polity Press
65 Bridge Street
Cambridge CB2 1UR, UK

Polity Press
350 Main Street
Malden, MA 02148, USA

A catalogue record for this book is available from the British Library.

Library of Congress Cataloging-in-Publication Data

Bauman, Zygmunt.
  Identity: conversations with Benedetto Vecchi / Zygmunt Bauman.
    p. cm. – (Themes for the 21st century)
  Includes bibliographical references and index.
    ISBN 0-7456-3308-0 (alk. paper) – ISBN 0-7456-3309-9 (pbk.: alk.
paper)
    1. Identity. I. Vecchi, Benedetto. II. Title. III. Series.
  BD236 .B39 2004
  302.5′4–dc22

                                                              2003020403

Typeset in 10.5 on 12 pt Plantin
by Kolam Information Services Pvt. Ltd., Pondicherry, India.
Printed and bound in Great Britain by MPG Books, Bodmin, Cornwall

For further information on Polity, visit our website: www.polity.co.uk

Contents

Introduction
Benedetto Vecchi

In all his writings Zygmunt Bauman manages to unsettle our fundamental beliefs, and this book of interviews on the question of identity is no exception. The interviews were somewhat out of the ordinary in that they were not conducted with a tape recorder, and interviewer and interviewee never came face to face. E-mail was the chosen instrument for our dialogue, and it imposed a somewhat fragmentary rhythm to our exchange of questions and answers. In the absence of the time pressure associated with a head-to-head, our long-distance dialogue was marked by many pauses for reflection, requests for clarification, and minor deviations into matters we had not originally intended to explore. Every reply from Bauman only served to increase my sense of bewilderment. As the material he provided began to build up, I became increasingly aware that I had entered a much larger continent than I had previously expected and one whose maps were almost useless when it came to finding directions. This should come as no surprise, because Zygmunt Bauman is not like other sociologists or 'social scientists'. His reflections are work-in-progress, and he is never content with defining or 'conceptualizing' an event, but rather aims to

establish connections with social phenomena or manifestations of the public ethos that seem far removed from the
initial object of the investigation, and to comment on those
phenomena and manifestations. The following pages will
be more than sufficient to demonstrate this roving nature
of his reflections, which makes it impossible to establish
his intellectual influences or his membership of any particular school of thought.

Zygmunt Bauman has often been defined as an eclectic
sociologist, and he would certainly take no offence at such
a definition. Nevertheless the methodology he brings to
bear on a subject aims above all to 'reveal' the myriad
connections between the object under investigation and
other manifestations of life in human society. Indeed, this
sociologist of Polish origin finds it essential to gather the
'truth' of every feeling, lifestyle and collective behaviour.
This is only possible if you analyse the social, cultural and
political context in which a particular phenomenon exists
as well as the phenomenon itself. Hence the roving nature
of his thoughts throughout his works which study subjects
ranging from the crisis in public debate in *In Search of
Politics* (1999) to the changing role of intellectuals in a
society based on attention-seeking in *Legislators and Inter-
preters: On Modernity, Postmodernity and Intellectuals*
(1987). His intellect is, in fact, both restive and rigorous;
it is true to the present, but careful to acknowledge its
genealogy, or rather genealogies.

On this occasion, the subject was identity, a subject that
is by its very nature elusive and ambivalent. Bauman faced
up to the challenge and performed a double somersault: he
reread the history of modern sociology in the light of the
obsession and importance with which current public
debate treats identity, and reached the conclusion that it
is better not to look for reassuring responses in the 'established texts' of critical thought. *Liquid Modernity* (2000)

projects us into a world in which everything is elusive, where the anguish, pain and insecurity caused by 'living in society' require a patient and ongoing examination of reality and how individuals are 'placed' within it. Any attempt to placate the inconstancy and precariousness of the plans men and women make for their lives and thus explain this sense of disorientation by parading past certainties and established texts would be as futile as attempting to empty the ocean with a bucket.

We have here an intellectual who considers the principle of responsibility to be the first act of any involvement in public life. For a sociologist this means perceiving sociology not as a discipline 'separate' from other fields of knowledge, but as providing the analytical tool to establish a lively interaction between it and philosophy, social psychology and narrative. We should not, therefore, find it strange if the documents on which he tests his penchant for 'short-circuiting' mass culture and high culture include articles from leading newspapers, advertising slogans and Søren Kierkegaard's philosophical reflections on Don Giovanni.

Although he is not keen to speak about his own life, it needs to be said that Zygmunt Bauman was born in 1925 into a Jewish family in Poland. Having escaped to the Soviet Union at the beginning of the Second World War, he joined the Polish army allied to the Red Army, and in it he fought Nazism. In his book *Conversations with Bauman* (2001) he tells us that he commenced his studies and degree in sociology on his return to Warsaw, and that his first teachers were Stanislaw Ossowski and Julian Hochfeld, two Polish intellectuals little known outside Poland but fundamental to his intellectual formation. Above all they gave him the ability 'to look the world in the face' without recourse to preconceived ideologies. If you ask Bauman, who became a leading figure in the Warsaw 'school of sociology', to describe the difficulties experienced during the 1950s and 1960s, he does so without any hostility to those who opposed his work. Indeed, he uses his subtle irony to compare the arduous academic freedom in Poland with European and American academic conformism. He is equally discreet about his role in the 'Polish October' of 1956, when he took part in the powerful reform movement that challenged the leading role of Polish United Workers' Party and the country's subjugation to Moscow's will. This experience marked Bauman and prepared him for his showdown with the official ideology of Soviet Marxism in which the works of Antonio Gramsci were to play their part. He started to make frequent trips abroad. He took a year's sabbatical at the London School of Economics, and attended many conferences in almost all Europe's great universities. Then came 1968, which was to prove a turning-point in his life. Bauman, who supported the fledgling Polish students' movement, had his works banned by the Communist Party when anti-Semitism was used to repress students and university teachers who demanded an end to single-party rule in the name of 'liberty, justice and equality'.

After he had been prevented from teaching, Zygmunt Bauman moved to England, where he still lives. In almost all his books, and particularly in *Modernity and the Holocaust* (1989), he expresses his enormous gratitude to Janina, his wife and life companion, to whom he is very close both emotionally and intellectually. She is perhaps one of the most important intellectual figures in Bauman's reflections first on 'solid modernity' and later on 'liquid modernity'.

His intellectual life in England, where he teaches at Leeds University, has been intensely productive. I have already referred to some of the works, but taken as a whole it is quite clear that with the publication of *Postmodern Ethics* (1993), Bauman started to concentrate on globalization, examining it not only from an economic point of view but also and primarily for its effects on daily life. Bauman, doyen of European sociology, took this as the starting point for his exploration of the 'new world' that has been created by the increasing interdependence on planet earth. This period produced such books as *Globalization: The Human Consequences* (1998), *Community* (2000), *The Individualized Society* (2001), *Liquid Modernity* (2000) and *Society under Siege* (2002) which constitute Bauman's great tableau on globalization as a radical and irreversible change. He perceives it as a 'great transformation' that has affected state structures, working conditions, interstate relations, collective subjectivity, cultural production, daily life and relations between the self and the other. This book of interviews on identity could be considered a small addition to this tableau. To paraphrase one of his replies on identity, we can confidently assert that globalization, or rather 'liquid modernity', is not a puzzle that can be put together on the basis of a pre-established model. If anything, it should be seen as a process, as should its understanding and analysis; as should identity that asserts itself in the crisis of multiculturalism, or in Islamic fundamentalism, or when the internet facilitates the expression of off-the-peg identities.

The question of identity is associated too with the breakdown of the welfare state and the subsequent growth in a sense of insecurity, with the 'corrosion of character' that insecurity and flexibility in the workplace have produced in society. The conditions are created for a hollowing out of democratic institutions and a privatization of the public sphere, which increasingly resembles a talk show where everyone shouts out their own justifications without ever managing to affect the injustice and lack of freedom existing in the modern world.

However the 'corrosion of character' that figures so prominently in Bauman's most recent works is simply the most striking manifestation of the profound anxiety that typifies the behaviour, decision-making and life projects of men and women in Western society. As an intellectual who experienced the horrors of the twentieth century – war, the persecution of Jews and exile from 'his' country so as to remain loyal to himself – Bauman knows very well the difference between long-term phenomena and contingent expressions of a 'long transformation', which globalization clearly is. It is essential to understand the prominent features of a 'long transition' in order to identify social trends, but it is equally necessary to contextualize manifestations of social existence within the long period. This is perhaps why Bauman on several occasions gently mocks those who attempt to conceptualize definitively the political relevance of identity. In a society that has made social, cultural and sexual identities uncertain and transient, any attempt to 'firm up' that which has become liquid through a politics of identity would inevitably lead critical thought up a blind alley. His is therefore an invitation to exercise a little wisdom, but this will inevitably be disrupted by unexpected guests, namely those strategies for adaptation to 'liquid modernity' that we see at work in late capitalist societies. Discussion on identity is therefore a socially necessary convention that is used with extreme nonchalance to mould and give substance to off-the-peg biographies. We talk of identity because of the collapse of those institutions that, to use one of Georg Simmel's famous expressions, constituted for many years the premises upon which modern society was built.

In *Community* Zygmunt Bauman investigated the ambivalence required by the new social ties that are brought about in late capitalist society. They can give rise to demands for protection and a return to a familiar and restricted world that creates boundaries and barriers that hold the 'outsider' at bay, whoever he or she might be. At the same time, however, the community represents a shelter in relation to the planet-wide effects of globalization, as we can clearly see from the crisis that the melting pot is currently undergoing in the United States. It is as dangerous to ignore this as it is to appease it. It seems to me that the same is true of the politics of identity. It is well known that Bauman has often drawn attention to the gilded cosmopolitanism and seductive mobility of the global elites and how these contrast with the misery of those who cannot escape the local dimension. The politics of identity therefore speaks the language of those who have been marginalized by globalization. Yet many of those involved in postcolonial studies emphasize that recourse to identity should be considered an ongoing process of redefining oneself and of the invention and reinvention of one's own history. This is where we find the ambivalence of identity: nostalgia for the past together with complete accordance with 'liquid modernity'. It is this that creates the possibility of overturning the planetary effects of globalization and using them in a positive manner. Those who would define this operation as 'optimism of thought and pessimism of the will' would not in fact be mistaken. Through the breakdown in the social bonds of 'solid modernity' it is possible to glimpse a scenario leading towards social liberation.

True to his roots in the great European tradition of sociology, Bauman underscores the risks involved in this kind of discourse. Nevertheless it is a risk that has to be run, precisely because the question of identity needs to concern itself once again with what it really is: a socially necessary convention. If not, it is certain that the politics of identity will dominate the world stage, a danger of which we have already had plenty of warning signs. Ultimately, the various religious fundamentalisms are nothing more than the transposition of identity on to politics by cynical apprentice magicians. The deception behind this transposition can only be uncovered if you reconstruct the crossover from the individual dimension, which identity always has, to its codification as a social convention. This, I believe, is the central question.

Whatever the field of investigation in which the ambivalence of identity is tested, it is always essential to perceive the twin poles that it imposes on social existence: oppression and liberation. This mysterious circle needs to be broken. Bauman is rightly convinced that the truth can only be stated in the *agora*, thus removing the veil of obscurantism that prevents this same ambivalence from becoming the place where it is possible to experience one's own principle of responsibility. It might seem contradictory that this mild man, who is so keen to protect his privacy, should constantly entreat everyone to speak up, but it is an invitation that must be accepted even when public discussion will trigger bitter disagreements. This would be the exact opposite of the public prattling of endless and unchanging TV talk shows to which we have become so accustomed. The *agora* is the favoured space in which to speak out on such issues as the now unrestrained privatization of the public sphere, and it is this centrality that he assigns to it that makes Bauman one of the most lucid and sceptical critics of the prevailing zeitgeist during this period of liquid 'modernity'.

Identity

According to the old custom of Charles University of
Prague, the national anthem of the country to which the
person receiving an honorary doctorate belongs is played
during the conferment ceremony. When my turn to be
so honoured came, I was asked to choose between the
British and the Polish anthems . . . Well, I did not find an
answer easy.

Britain was the country of my choice and by which I was
chosen through an offer of a teaching job once I could no
longer stay in Poland, the country of my birth, because my
right to teach was taken away. But there, in Britain, I was
an immigrant, a newcomer – not so long ago a refugee
from a foreign country, an alien. I have since become a
naturalized British citizen, but once a newcomer can you
ever stop being a newcomer? I had no intention of passing
for an Englishman and neither my students nor my col-
leagues ever had any doubt that I was a foreigner, a Pole to
be exact. That tacit 'gentleman's agreement' prevented
our relations from going sour – on the contrary, it made
them honest, smooth, and on the whole cloudless and
friendly. So perhaps the Polish anthem should have been
played? But that would also mean acting on false pre-

tences: thirty-odd years before the Prague ceremony I had been stripped of Polish citizenship. My exclusion was official, initiated and confirmed by the power entitled to set apart the 'inside' from the 'outside', those who belong from those who don't – so the right to the Polish national anthem was no longer mine . . .

Janina, my lifelong companion and a person who had given a lot of thought to the traps and trials of self-definition (she was, after all, the author of a book under the title *Dream of Belonging*), found the solution: why not the European anthem? Indeed, why not? A European, no doubt, I was, had never stopped being – born in Europe, living in Europe, working in Europe, thinking European, feeling European; and what is more, there is thus far no European passport office with the authority to issue or to refuse a 'European passport', and so to confer or to deny our right to call ourselves Europeans.

Our decision to ask for the European anthem to be played was simultaneously 'inclusive' and 'exclusive'. It referred to an entity that embraced both alternative reference points of my identity, but at the same time cancelled out, as less relevant or irrelevant, the differences between them and so also a possible 'identity split'. It removed from the agenda an identity defined in terms of nationality – the kind of identity that has been barred and inaccessible to me. Poignant verses of the European anthem helped: *alle Menschen werden Brüder* . . . The image of 'brotherhood' is the epitome of squaring the circle: different yet the same, separate yet inseparable, independent yet joined.

I tell you of this little episode since it contained, in a nutshell, most of the vexing dilemmas and haunting choices that tend to make 'identity' a matter of grave concerns and hot controversies. Identity-seekers invariably face the daunting task of 'squaring a circle': that generic phrase, as you know, implies tasks that can never be completed in a 'real time', but are assumed to be able to reach completion in the fullness of time – in infinity...

It is common to say that 'communities' (to which identities refer as to entities that define them) are of two kinds. There are communities of life and fate whose members (according to Siegfried Kracauer's formula) 'live together in an indissoluble attachment', and communities that are 'welded together solely by ideas or various principles'.[1] Of the two kinds, the first has been denied to me – just as it has been and will be to a growing number of my contemporaries. If it were not denied, it would hardly occur to you to ask me about my identity; and if you did ask, I would not know what kind of answer you would expect from me. The question of identity arises only with the exposure to 'communities' of the second category – and it does so only because there is more than one idea to conjure up and hold together the 'communities welded by ideas' to which one is exposed in our variegated, polycultural world. It is because there are many such ideas and principles around which 'communities of believers' grow that one has to compare, to make choices, to make them repeatedly, to revise choices already made on another occasion, to try to reconcile contradictory and often incompatible demands. Julian Tuwim, the great Polish poet of Jewish ancestry, was known to remark that hating Polish anti-Semites more than anti-Semites of any other country was the strongest proof of his Polishness (I suppose that my Jewishness is confirmed by Israeli iniquities paining me still more than atrocities committed by other countries). One becomes aware that 'belonging' and 'identity' are not cut in rock, that they are not secured by a lifelong guarantee, that they are eminently negotiable and revocable; and that one's own decisions, the steps one takes, the way one acts – and the determination to stick by all that – are crucial factors of both. In other words, the thought of 'having an identity' will not occur to people as long as 'belonging' remains their fate, a condition with no alternative. They will begin to entertain such a thought only in the form of a task to be performed, and to be performed over and over again rather than in a one-off fashion.

I do not remember paying much attention to the question of 'my identity', at least the national part of it, before the brutal awakening of March 1968 when my Polishness was publicly cast in doubt. I guess that until then I expected, matter-of-factly, and without any soul-searching or calculating, to retire when the time came from the University of Warsaw, and be buried when the time came at one of Warsaw's cemeteries. But since March 1968 I have been and still am expected by everyone around to self-define and I am supposed to have a considered, carefully balanced, keenly argued view of my identity. Why? Because once I had been set in motion, pulled out from wherever could pass for my 'natural habitat', there was no place where I could be seen as fitting in, as they say, one hundred per cent. In each and every place I was – sometimes slightly, at some other times blatantly – 'out of place'.

It so happened that in the bunch of problems called 'my identity', nationality has been given particular prominence; I share that lot with millions of refugees and migrants, whom our fast globalizing world turns out on a fast accelerating scale. But finding identity to be a bunch of problems rather than a single-issue campaign is a feature I share with a much greater number, practically with all men and women of the 'liquid modern' era.

The peculiarities of my biography have only dramatized and brought into full view the kind of condition which is nowadays quite common and on the way to becoming almost universal. In our liquid modern times the world around us is sliced into poorly coordinated fragments while our individual lives are cut into a succession of ill-connected episodes. Few if any of us can avoid the passage through more than one genuine or putative, well-integrated or ephemeral 'community of ideas and principles', so most of us have trouble with resolving (to use Paul Ricoeur's terms) the issue of *la mêmete* (the consistency and continuity of our identity over time). Few if any of us are exposed to just one 'community of ideas and principles' at a time, and so most of us have similar trouble with the issue of *l'ipséite* (coherence of whatever distinguishes us as persons). My colleague and friend, Agnes Heller, with whom I share to quite a degree a life predicament, complained once that being a woman, a Hungarian, a Jew, an American, a philosopher, she was saddled with rather too many identities for one person. Well, she could easily extend the list – but the frames of reference she named are already numerous enough to demonstrate the awesome complexity of the task.

To be wholly or in part 'out of place' everywhere, not to be completely anywhere (that is without qualifications and caveats, without some aspects of oneself 'sticking out' and seen by others as looking odd) may be an upsetting, sometimes annoying experience. There is always something to explain, to apologize for, to hide or on the contrary to boldly display, to negotiate, to bid for and to bargain for; there are differences to be smoothed or glossed over, or to be on the contrary made more salient and legible. 'Identities' float in the air, some of one's own choice but others inflated and launched by those around, and one needs to be constantly on the alert to defend the first against the second; there is a heightened likelihood of misunderstanding, and the outcome of the negotiation forever hangs in the balance. The more one practises and masters the difficult skills needed to get by in such an admittedly ambivalent condition, the less sharp and hurting the rough edges feel, the less overwhelming the challenges and the less irksome the effects. One can even begin to feel everywhere *chez soi*, 'at home' – but the price to be paid is to accept that nowhere will one be fully and truly at home.

One can resent all these discomforts and (hoping against hope) seek redemption, or at least respite, in a dream of belonging. But one can also make a vocation, a mission, a consciously chosen destiny out of one's fate of no choice – all the more so because of the benefits that such a decision may bring to those who take it and see it through, and for the sake of the likely benefits they may then offer to other people around.

Ludwig Wittgenstein famously declared that the best places in which to resolve philosophical problems are railway stations (remember that he had no first-hand experience of airports . . .). One of the greatest in the long chain of exquisite Spanish-language writers, Juan Goytisolo, who moved through Paris and the United States to settle in Morocco, summed up his life experience in the observation that 'intimacy and distance create a privileged situation. Both are necessary.' Jacques Derrida, one of the greatest philosophers of our liquid modern era, in perpetual exile since the Vichy government expelled him from his local French school as a twelve-year-old Jewish boy, by common opinion built his impressive philosophical home on 'cultural crossroads'. George Steiner, an acute and most insightful cultural critic, named Samuel Beckett, Jorge Luis Borges and Vladimir Nabokov as the greatest contemporary writers; what in his view united the three otherwise sharply distinct authors and made them tower above the rest was that they all moved with ease in several different linguistic universes. That continuous boundary-transgression allowed them to spy out human invention and ingenuity behind the stony and solemn facades of seemingly timeless and indomitable creeds, and so gave

them the courage needed to join in cultural creation know-
ingly, aware of the risks and pitfalls that notoriously mark
all boundless expanses.

Of Georg Simmel, from whom I learned more than from
any other sociologist and whose way of doing sociology has
been for me (and, I guess, will remain to the end) the
ultimate (though alas unattainable) ideal, Kracauer rightly
observed that one of the fundamental aims that guided his
life's work was 'to rid every *geistige* [spiritual, intellectual]
phenomenon of its false being-unto-itself and show how it
is embedded in the larger context of life'. In the centre of
Simmel's vision, and so of his world and his understanding
of his own place in that world, always stood the human
individual – 'considered as bearer of culture and as a
mature *geistige* being, acting and evaluating in full control
of the powers of his soul and linked to his fellow human
beings in collective action and feeling'. If you keep prod-
ding me to declare my identity (that is, my 'postulated
self', the horizon towards which I strive and by which I
assess, censure and correct my moves), this is as far as and
no further than you can push me. This is as close as I may
come . . .

BENEDETTO VECCHI   *In the sociological imagination identity always is something very evasive and slippery, almost an a priori, that is, a pre-existing reality.
For example, in Émile Durkheim, collective identities always remain in the
background, but there is no doubt that in his most famous book, The Division
of Labour in Society, the division of labour is a contradictory element. On one
hand, it puts social ties at risk, but at the same time it acts as a factor of
stabilization in the transition towards the creation of a new social order.
However, in this analytical frame, identity is to be considered as an objective,
an aim, rather than a predefined factor. What's your opinion?*

My opinion is the same as yours . . . Yes, indeed, 'identity'
is revealed to us only as something to be invented rather
than discovered; as a target of an effort, 'an objective'; as

something one still needs to build from scratch or to choose from alternative offers and then to struggle for and then to protect through yet more struggle – though for the struggle to be victorious, the truth of the precarious and forever incomplete status of identity needs to be, and tends to be, suppressed and laboriously covered up.

Today this truth is more difficult to hide than it used to be at the beginning of the modern era. The agencies most determined to conceal it have lost interest; they retreat from the battlefield and are glad to leave the chores of finding or constructing an identity to us, individual men and women, singly or severally, rather than jointly. The frailty and the forever provisional status of identity can no longer be concealed. The secret is out. But this is a new, quite recent development.

I wonder therefore whether it is fair to ask the spiritual fathers of sociology, be it Weber or Durkheim, or even Simmel, who was the most farsighted and ran further ahead of his time than all the rest, to instruct us what and how to think of an issue that burst into our shared awareness and settled there long after their death. They were all engaged in a conversation with the troubles, worries and concerns of men and women of their times (the profundity, earnestness and dedication of that engagement was their true greatness and their most important legacy for later sociology); 'identity' was not prominent among those concerns. I suppose that were they to have turned their ears, finely tuned to whatever might be the great issues of their own time, to our kind of society that was to be born almost a century later, they would have considered the sudden centrality of the 'problem of identity' in the learned debates as well as in common consciousness a most intriguing sociological puzzle.

It is indeed a puzzle and a challenge to sociology – if you recall that only a few decades ago 'identity' was nowhere near the centre of our thoughts, remaining but an object of philosophical meditation. Today, though, 'identity' is 'the loudest talk in town', the burning issue on everybody's mind and tongue. It would be this sudden fascination with identity, rather than identity itself, that would draw the attention of the classics of sociology were they to have lived long enough to confront it. They would probably take a hint from Martin Heidegger (but they were no longer around even when that clue was offered): you tend to notice things and put them into the focus of your scrutiny and contemplation only when they vanish, go bust, start to behave oddly or otherwise let you down.

Just before the outbreak of the last world war a census of population was conducted in my native Poland. Poland was then a multi-ethnic society. Certain parts of the country were populated by a bizarre mixture of ethnic groups, religious faiths, customs and languages. Reforging that mixture, through forcible conversion and assimilation, into a uniform or nearly uniform nation after, say, the French model was perhaps a goal energetically pursued by a part of the Polish political elite, yet it was by no means a universally accepted and consistently followed objective, let alone a project anywhere near completion.

As one would expect in a modern state, its census commissioners were nevertheless trained to expect that for every human being there must be a nation to which he or she belonged. They were briefed to collect information about the national self-assignment of every subject of the Polish state (you would say today: his or her 'national or ethnic identity'). In about a million cases the commissioners failed; the people they questioned simply could not grasp what a 'nation' was and what 'having a nationality' was like. Despite the pressure – the threats of a fine combined with truly Herculean efforts to explain the meaning of 'nationality' – they stubbornly stuck to the sole answers which made sense to them: 'we are locals', 'we are of this place', 'we are from here', 'we belong here'. The administrators of the census had to surrender in the end and add 'the locals' to the official list of nations.

Poland was by no means a unique case; neither was it to be the last case of that kind on record. Quite a few years later a French research study showed that after two centuries of strenuous nation-building, 'le pays' was for many French country folk only twenty kilometres in diameter, give or take another five...As Philippe Robert recently pointed out, 'for most of the history of human societies, social relations have stayed enclosed firmly in the realm of proximity.'[2] Remember that in the eighteenth century the journey from, say, Paris to Marseille took as long as it did in the Roman Empire. For most people, 'society' as the uppermost 'totality' of human cohabitation (if they thought in such terms at all) was equal to the immediate neighbourhood. 'One could speak of a society of mutual acquaintance,' Robert suggests. Inside that network of familiarity from the cradle to the coffin, each person's place was too evident to be pondered, let alone negotiated. Any unclarity in such matters (as in the case of the relatively few 'masterless people' who took off along the equally masterless roads having found no livelihood in their native communities) was a marginal phenomenon and a minor worry, easily dealt with and resolved by ad hoc measures along the lines of the *maréchaussée*, the corps of mounted constabulary that was the first police force in Western history. It took the slow disintegration and shrinking of the holding power of neighbourhoods, supplemented by the transport revolution, to clear the site for identity to be born: as a *problem* and, first and foremost, a *task*. The margins swelled rapidly, invading the core areas of human cohabitation. Suddenly, the question of identity needed to be asked – since no obvious answer was on offer.

The nascent modern state that faced the need to create an order no longer automatically reproduced by the well-settled and closely knit 'societies of mutual familiarity' annexed that question and deployed it in its job of laying the foundations of its novel and unfamiliar legitimacy claims.

It seemed natural to suppose that following its rapid expansion, the 'identity problem' would best be tackled by a parallel expansion of order-monitoring labours like those practised and tested by the *maréchaussée*. The nation-state, as Giorgio Agamben has observed, is a state that makes 'nativity or birth' the 'foundation of its own sovereignty'. 'The fiction that is implicit here', Agamben points out, 'is that *birth* [*nascita*] comes into being immediately as *nation*, so that there may not be any difference between the two moments.'[3] The hapless targets of the Polish census inquiry simply failed to absorb that fiction as a self-evident 'fact of the matter'. They were astonished to hear that one should have a 'national identity' and that one could be asked what that nationality was.

Not that they were particularly dense and unimaginative people. After all, asking 'who you are' makes sense to you only once you believe that you can be someone other than you are; only if you have a choice, and only if it depends on you what you choose; only if you have to do something, that is, for the choice to be 'real' and to hold. But this is precisely what did not occur to the residents of the backwater villages and forest settlements – who never had a chance to think of moving places, let alone to seek, discover or invent something as nebulous (indeed, as unthinkable) as 'another identity'. Their way of being-in-the-world stripped the question of 'identity' of the meaning made obvious by other ways of life – ways that our linguistic usages prompt us to call 'modern'.

Jorge Luis Borges would describe the plight of the molested 'locals' as a case of people who are presented with a task 'that is not forbidden to other men, but forbidden' to them – just as happened to Averroes when he strove to translate Aristotle into Arabic. 'Bounded within the circle of Islam' and thus 'trying to imagine what a play is without ever having suspected what a theatre is', Averroes 'could never know the meaning of *tragedy* and *comedy*'.[4]

The idea of 'identity', and a 'national identity' in particular, did not gestate and incubate in human experience 'naturally', did not emerge out of that experience as a self-evident 'fact of life'. That idea was *forced* into the *Lebenswelt* of modern men and women – and arrived as a *fiction*. It congealed into a 'fact', a 'given', precisely because it had been a *fiction*, and thanks to the painfully felt gap which stretched between what that idea implied, insinuated or prompted, and the *status quo ante* (the state of affairs preceding, and innocent of, human intervention). *The idea of 'identity' was born out of the crisis of belonging* and out of the effort it triggered to bridge the gap between the 'ought' and the 'is' and to lift reality to the standards set by the idea – to remake the reality in the likeness of the idea.

Identity could only enter the *Lebenswelt* as a task, as an *as-yet-unfulfilled, unfinished task*, a clarion call, a duty and an urge to act – and the nascent modern state did whatever it took to make such a duty obligatory for all people inside its territorial sovereignty. Identity born as fiction needed a lot of coercing and convincing to harden and coagulate into a reality (more correctly: into the sole reality thinkable) – and the story of the birth and maturation of the modern state was overflown with both.

The fiction of the 'nativity of birth' played the principal role among the formulae deployed by the nascent modern state to legitimate its demand for the unconditional subordination of its subjects (somehow, curiously, overlooked by Max Weber in his typology of legitimations). State and nation needed each other; their marriage, one is tempted to say, was made in heaven . . . The state sought the obedience of its subjects by representing itself as the fulfilment of the nation's destiny and a guarantee of its continuation. On the other hand, a nation without a state would be bound to be unsure of its past, insecure in its present and uncertain of its future, and so doomed to a precarious existence. Were it not for the state's power to define, classify, segregate, separate and select, the aggregate of local traditions, dialects, customary laws and ways of life would hardly be recast into anything like the postulated unity and cohesion of a national community. If the state was the fulfilment of the nation's destiny, it was also a necessary condition of there being a nation claiming – loudly, confidently and effectively – a shared destiny. The rule *cuius regio, eius natio* (he who rules decides the nationality) cut both ways . . .

'National identity' was from the start, and remained for a long time, an *agonistic* notion and a battle cry. A cohesive national community overlapping with the aggregate of state subjects was destined to remain not just perpetually unaccomplished, but forever precarious; a *project* calling for continuous vigilance, gigantic effort and the application of a lot of force to make sure that the call is heard and obeyed (Ernest Renan called the nation 'a daily plebiscite' – despite speaking from the experience of the French state known at least since the Napoleonic era for its uniquely centralistic ambitions). None of such conditions would be met if it were not for the overlapping of the domicile territory with the undivided sovereignty of the state – which, as Agamben (following Carl Schmitt) suggests, consists first and foremost in the power of *exemption*. Its *raison d'être* was the drawing, tightening and policing of the boundary between 'us' and 'them'. 'Belonging' would have lost its lustre and seductive power together with its

integrating/disciplining function had it not been consistently selective and constantly given flesh and reinvigorated
by the threat and practice of exclusion.

National identity, let me add, was never like other identities. Unlike other identities that did not demand unequivocal allegiance and exclusive fidelity, national
identity would not recognize competition, let alone an
opposition. National identity painstakingly construed by
the state and its agencies (or 'shadow governments' or
'governments in exile' in the case of aspiring nations –
'nations *in spe*', only clamouring for a state of their own)
aimed at the monopolistic right to draw the boundary
between 'us' and 'them'. Short of monopoly, states pursued the unassailable positions of supreme courts passing
the binding, no-appeal-allowed sentences on the claims of
litigating identities.

Just as the state's laws overrode all other customary
forms of justice and made them null and void in cases of
a clash, national identity would allow or tolerate only such
other identities as would not be suspected of colliding
(whether in principle or on occasion) with the unqualified
priority of national loyalty. Being the subject of a state
was the sole feature authoritatively confirmed in identity
cards and passports. Other, 'smaller' identities were en-
couraged and/or obliged to seek endorsement-followed-
by-protection from the state-authorized offices, and
thereby to obliquely confirm the superiority of 'national
identity' through relying on royal or republican charters,
state diplomas and state-endorsed certificates. Whoever
else you might have been or have aspired to become, it
was the 'appropriate institutions' of the state that had the
final word. An uncertified identity was a fraud; its carrier
was a false pretender – a conman.

The severity of the demands was a reflection of
the endemic and incurable precariousness of the nation-

building-and-maintenance task. Let me repeat: the 'natur-alness' of the assumption that 'belonging-through-birth' meant, automatically and unequivocally, belonging to a *nation* was a laboriously construed convention; the appear-ance of 'naturalness' could be anything but 'natural'. Unlike the 'mini-societies of mutual familiarity', those localities in which the lives of most men and women of the premodern and premobility times were spent from cradle to grave, 'nation' was an imagined entity that could enter the *Lebenswelt* only if mediated by the artifice of a concept. The appearance of naturalness, and so also the credibility of the asserted belonging, could be only an end-product of protracted past battles; and its perpetu-ation could not be guaranteed except through the battles yet to come.

In Italy, you must know it only too well . . . Two centur-ies after the victory of the Risorgimento Italy is hardly a country with one language and fully integrated local con-cerns. Time and again a call is made to allow local interests to override the (accused of being artificial) national bonds. The priority of the national identity is still, as it was before the unification, an open and hotly contested question. As Jonathan Matthew Schwartz aptly puts it, rather than the totality being greater than the sum of its parts (as Durkheim, trusting state power to fulfil its ambitions, insisted), 'the imagined whole is indeed more fictive than the sum of its parts.'[5]

One who certainly takes a distance from this formulation is Georg Simmel. In his essays on forms of life in metropolises and the conflict of modern society, identity is mentioned precisely as an expression of institutions such as Family, State, Church, which are – in a Kantian perspective – the a priori of social life. In this case, the element of identity is almost disintegrated by modern mass society. In fact, Simmel focuses quite willingly on the forms of life which have emerged from the dissolution of established orders. However, if we confront the *analyses of the German sociologist with those of Durkheim, identity is a minor element in the analysis of reality. Don't you agree?*

I repeat what I suggested before: there are weighty reasons *not* to seek answers to our 'identity problems' in the work of the founding fathers, even in the work of Georg Simmel, who due to the peculiarities of his biography could glimpse and taste the kind of existential condition which was only much later to become everybody's fate – blessing or curse.

The main reason why the founders of modern sociology cannot answer the questions posited by our present plight is that if the 'problem of identity' a hundred or more years ago was given shape by the operation of a *cuius regio, eius natio* principle, today's 'identity problems' stem, on the contrary, from the *abandonment* of that principle or from the half-heartedness of its application and the ineffectiveness of its promotion where such promotion is attempted. Once identity loses the *social* anchors that made it look 'natural', predetermined and non-negotiable, 'identification' becomes ever more important for the individuals desperately seeking a 'we' to which they may bid for access. As Lars Dencik, writing from the Scandinavian experience, put it:

> Social affiliations – more or less inherited – that are trad-
> itionally ascribed to individuals as a definition of identity:
> race . . . gender, country or place of birth, family and social
> class, are now . . . becoming less important, diluted and
> altered, in the most technologically and economically ad-
> vanced countries. At the same time, there is a longing for,
> and attempts to find or establish new groups to which one
> experiences belonging and which can facilitate identity-
> making. An increasing feeling of insecurity follows . . .[6]

Let me point out already at this stage (hoping for a later opportunity to discuss the matter in more detail, as it deserves) that the 'groups' which the individuals bereaved by the orthodox frames of reference 'attempt to find or establish' tend to be nowadays electronically mediated, frail 'virtual totalities', easy to enter and easy to abandon. They are hardly a valid substitution for the solid, and pretending to be yet more solid, forms of togetherness that thanks to their genuine or putative solidity could promise that comforting (even if deceptive or fraudulent) 'we feeling' – not offered by 'surfing the net'. To quote Clifford Stoll, a self-confessed, though by now cured and recovered internet addict: preoccupied with chasing and catching the 'join now!' offers flashing on computer screens, we are losing the ability to enter into spontaneous interaction with real people.[7] Charles Handy, a management theorist, concurs: 'fun they may be, these virtual communities, but they create only an illusion of intimacy and a pretense of community.'[8] They are not valid substitutes for 'getting your knees under the table, seeing people's faces, and having real conversation'. Neither can such 'virtual communities' give substance to personal identity – the primary reason to seek them out. If anything, they make coming to terms with one's own self more difficult than it otherwise would be.

In the words of Andy Hargreaves, professor of education and a uniquely perceptive observer of the contemporary cultural scene:

> In airports and other public spaces, people with mobile-phone headset attachments walk around, talking aloud and alone, like paranoid schizophrenics, oblivious to their immediate surroundings. Introspection is a disappearing act. Faced with moments alone in their cars, on the street or at the supermarket checkouts, more and more people do not collect their thoughts, but scan their mobile phone messages for shreds of evidence that someone, somewhere, may need or want them.[9]

Georg Simmel's strollers of the city streets were famous for their 'blasé' attitude. They did not carry mobile telephone headsets, though. Just like us now, they might have been avid spectators of the urban street dramas, but they visited that theatre without joining its company. They took distance from what they saw and watched. It was not a simple matter, though, for them to keep their distance from the stage on which the drama unravelled: physical proximity could easily be confused with spiritual proximity. Erving Goffman tried to compose an inventory of 'civil inattention' stratagems – the multitude of inconspicuous, petty yet intricate gestures and body movements to which each of us resorts matter-of-factly whenever we find ourselves among strangers, and which signal our intention to stay detached, uninvolved, and keep our own company and counsel. Simmel's urban strollers, and the later Baudelaire/Foucault *flâneurs* and Goffman's practitioners of the art of civil inattention, did not walk the city streets in search of a community with which they could identify. The communal embodiment of identity, though, the 'someones' who 'need them and want them' and whom they need and want in exchange, waited for them, sedentary and in a more or less ready-to-serve and ready-to-use form, securely ensconced in family homes or workplaces.

This is where we, the denizens of a liquid modern world, differ. We seek and construct and keep together the communal references of our identities while *on the move* – struggling to match the similarly mobile, fast moving groups we seek and construct and try to keep alive for a moment, but not much longer. To do so, we don't need to study and master Goffman's code. Mobile phones will do. We can buy them, complete with all the skills we may need for the purpose, in a high-street shop. With a headset attachment securely in place, we parade our detachment from the street we walk, no longer needing the elaborate etiquette. Switching on the mobile, we switch off the street. Physical proximity no longer collides with spiritual remoteness.

With the world going at high speed and accelerating, you can no longer trust such frames of reference as claim utility on the grounds of their presumed durability (not to mention timelessness!). You neither trust them, nor need them, to be sure. Such frames do not easily take in new contents. They would soon prove to be much too poky and unwieldy to accommodate all those new, unexplored and untested identities that are temptingly within your reach, each one offering exciting since unfamiliar, and promising since so far un-discredited, benefits. The frames, stiff and sticky as they are, are also difficult to clean of old contents and shake them off once their 'use-by date' comes. In the brave new world of fleeting chances and frail securities, the old-style stiff and non-negotiable identities simply won't do.

Popular wisdom was quick to note the changing requirements, and promptly derided the received wisdom that was blatantly unfit to meet them. In 1994, a poster put up on the streets of Berlin poked fun at loyalties to frames no longer able to contain the world's realities: 'Your Christ is a Jew. Your car is Japanese. Your pizza is Italian. Your democracy – Greek. Your coffee – Brazilian. Your holiday – Turkish. Your numbers – Arabic. Your letters – Latin. Only your neighbour is a foreigner.'[10] In the nation-building era in Poland, children used to be drilled to offer the following answers to questions of identity: Who are you? A little Pole. What is your sign? White Eagle. Today's answers, suggests Monika Kostera, an eminent sociologist of contemporary culture, would run rather differently: Who are you? A handsome man in his forties, with a sense of humour. What is your sign? Gemini.[11]

The Berlin poster implies globalization, whereas the change in the likely answer to the 'who are you?' question

signals the collapse of the (genuine or postulated) hierarchy of identities. The two phenomena are closely
related.

Globalization means that the state no longer has the
clout or the wish to keep its marriage with the nation
rock-solid and impregnable. Extramarital flirts and even
adulterous affairs are both unavoidable and permissible,
often earnestly and keenly procured (following the prelim-
inary conditions set for their admission to the 'free world' –
first the OECD, then the European Union – the governments of East-Central Europe have opened their national
assets to global capital and dismantled all barriers to the
free flow of global finances). Having ceded most of their
labour-and-capital intensive tasks to global markets, states
have much less need for supplies of patriotic fervour. Even
patriotic sentiments, that most jealously guarded asset of
modern nation-states, have been ceded to market forces
and redeployed by them to beef up the profits of the
promoters of sport, show business, anniversary festivities
and the memorabilia industry. At the other end, seekers
after identities can expect little reassurance, let alone foolproof guarantees, from the state powers left with but
meagre remnants of their once indomitable and indivisible
territorial sovereignty. To recall Thomas Marshall's
famous triad of rights: economic rights are now out of
the state's hands, such political rights as states may offer
are strictly limited and kept inside of what Pierre Bourdieu
baptised the *pensée unique* of the thoroughly deregulated
free market neoliberal style, while social rights are replaced
one by one by the individual duty of self-care and one-
upmanship.

And so both partners in the nation-state wedlock grow
increasingly lukewarm about their marriage and drift,
slowly yet steadily, towards the now fashionable life-
political pattern of SDCs ('semi-detached couples').

No longer monitored and protected, galvanized and invigorated by monopoly-seeking institutions – exposed instead to a free play of competitive forces – any hierarchies or pecking orders of identities, and particularly solid and durable hierarchies and pecking orders, are neither sought nor easy to construct. The main reasons for identities to be sharply defined and unambiguous (as sharply defined and unequivocal as the state's territorial sovereignty), and to retain the same recognizable shape over time, have vanished or lost much of their once compelling power. Identities were given a free run; and it is now up to individual men and women to catch them in flight, using their own wits and tools.

Longing for identity comes from the desire for security, itself an ambiguous feeling. However exhilarating it may be in the short run, however full of promises and vague premonitions of an as yet untried experience, floating without support in a poorly defined space, in a stubbornly, vexingly 'betwixt-and-between' location, becomes in the long run an unnerving and anxiety-prone condition. On the other hand, a fixed position amidst the infinity of possibilities is not an attractive prospect either. In our liquid modern times, when the free-floating, unencumbered individual is the popular hero, 'being fixed' – being 'identified' inflexibly and without retreat – gets an increasingly bad press.

In the 'Living' columns of one of the most prestigious English newspapers you could read a few months ago the words of a respected 'relationships expert' informing you that 'when committing yourself, however half-heartedly, remember that you are likely to be closing the door to other romantic possibilities which may be more satisfying and fulfilling.' Another counsellor sounded blunter still: 'Promises of commitment are meaningless in the long term . . . Like other investments, they wax and wane.' And so, if you wish 'to relate', 'to belong' for the sake of your safety – keep your distance; if you expect and wish for fulfilment from your togetherness, do not make or demand commitments. Keep all doors open, all the time.

The abundance of engagements on offer, but even more the evident frailty of each one, does not inspire trust in long-term investments at the level of personal, intimate relationships. Neither does it inspire confidence in the place of work, where social status used to be defined and where livings continue to be earned and entitlements to personal dignity and social respect continue to be gained or lost. In a recent article Richard Sennett points out that 'a flexible workplace is unlikely to be a spot in which one would wish to build a nest.'[12] At the same time, with the average duration of a work ('project') contract in the most advanced, high-tech outfits in places like the much admired Silicon Valley at about eight months, such group solidarity as used to provide the breeding ground for democracy does not have time to take root and mature. There is little reason to expect one's loyalty to a group or an organization to be reciprocated. It is unwise ('irrational') to proffer such loyalty on credit when it is unlikely to be repaid.

To sum up: 'to identify oneself with . . . ' means to give hostages to an unknown fate which one cannot influence, let alone control. Perhaps it is wiser therefore to wear identities in the way Richard Baxter, the Puritan preacher quoted by Max Weber, proposed earthly riches to be worn: like a light cloak ready to be taken off at any time. Locations where the feeling of belonging was traditionally invested (job, family, neighbourhood) are either not available, or untrustworthy when they are, and so unlikely to quench the thirst for togetherness or placate the fear of loneliness and abandonment.

Hence the growing demand for what may be called 'cloakroom communities' – conjured into being, if in apparition only, by hanging up individual troubles, as theatregoers do with their coats, in one room. Any hyped or shocking event may provide an occasion to do so: a new public enemy promoted to number one position, an exciting football contest, a particularly 'photo-opportune', clever or cruel crime, the first showing of a heavily hyped film, or a marriage, divorce or misfortune of a celebrity currently in the limelight. Cloakroom communities are patched together for the duration of the spectacle and promptly dismantled again once the spectators collect their coats from the hooks in the cloakroom. Their advantage over the 'genuine stuff' is precisely their short lifespan and the pettiness of the commitment required to join and (however briefly) enjoy them. But they differ from the dreamt-of warm and solidary community in the way the mass copies on sale in a high-street department store differ from the haute couture originals ...

When the quality lets you down or is not available, you tend to seek redemption in quantity. If commitments, and so also commitments to any particular identity, are (as the expert quoted above authoritatively proclaimed) 'meaningless', you are inclined to swap one identity, chosen once and or all, for a 'network of connections'. Once you have done it, however, entering a commitment and making it secure appear even more difficult (and so more off-putting, even frightening) than before. You now miss the skills that would or at least could make it work. Being on the move, once a privilege and an achievement, is then no longer a matter of choice: it now becomes 'a must'. Keeping up the speed, once an exhilarating adventure, turns into an exhausting chore. Most importantly, that nasty uncertainty and that vexing confusion, which you hoped to have shaken off thanks to your speed, refuse to go. The facility for disengagement and termination-on-demand does not reduce the risks; it only distributes them, together with the anxieties they exhale, differently.

In our world of rampant 'individualization', identities
are mixed blessings. They vacillate between a dream and a
nightmare, and there is no telling when one will turn into
the other. At most times the two liquid modern modalities
of identity cohabit, even when located at different levels of
consciousness. In a liquid modern setting of life, identities
are perhaps the most common, most acute, most deeply
felt and troublesome incarnations of *ambivalence*. This is, I
would argue, why they are firmly placed at the very heart
of liquid modern individuals' attention and perched at the
top of their life agendas.

*During the first twenty years of the twentieth century the Marxist analysis of
social classes flourishes. From Gyorgy Lukács to Walter Benjamin, many of the
Marxist intellectuals ask themselves questions about the relationship between a
social gathering together and social consciousness. In this case, it can be said as
well that identity is a category which certainly has no right of citizenship
in thought. Maybe there is one exception: Lukács. In* History and Class
Consciousness *he often refers to the proliferation of forms of life, ways of
being, as consequences of mass society. But it is doubtless because it expresses
a false consciousness that, in the Marxist left, identity starts to be a problem for
the first time. What do you think of this?*

The form taken by the 'intellectual Marxism' that swept
over the academic centres of Europe and America by
the late 1960s was thoroughly 'economistic', and in most
cases severely reductionist. In the seventies, which as Peter
Beilharz rightly points out were 'probably the heyday of
intellectual Marxism in the West', 'politics, ideology and
citizenship were all displaced or viewed as effects of the
primary motor of capitalist development and collapse.'[13]
This did not have to be so. Marx (to quote Beilharz once
more) was, after all, 'himself first a liberal, shifting from a
focus on poverty and the attendant image of the citizen
only eventually to the harder concept of exploitation,
where the implicitly masculine silhouette of the proletarian

replaces that of a citizen'. So the reduction of the ascendant Marxist theory to the hard core of economic determinism might not have been inevitable, but in its time it was, I would say, 'overdetermined'. A subtler and more nuanced, 'multi-factorial' image of society would not foot the bill of the day. It was precisely the comprehensiveness of an all-embracing, single-factor explanation for such bafflingly diverse suffering, uneasiness and anxiety – which only a truncated, reductionist and unidimensional version of Marx's legacy could deliver – that attracted a generation perplexed and confused by tides of discontent which could be neither predicted nor explained by the standard stories of development, progress, and progressive development. There was an overwhelming feeling of urgency, an impatience which only a theory that could be swallowed in one gulp and digested on the spot could, at least for a time, quench. This was probably not the one and only (and certainly not a sufficient) cause of the wide enthusiasm for a severely emaciated and simplified (vulgarized rather) version of Marx's vision, but it could be seen as a sort of a wide riverbed on which numerous other conscious and subconscious drives could converge, becoming its tributaries.

No single-factor model is likely ever to account for the complexity of the 'lived world' and embrace the totality of human experience. This general rule also applied to the truncated, shrunk and dessicated version of Marxism. This was not, though, the sole reason why the ascendancy of that version proved to be but a short-lived episode that came to an abrupt end as early as the 1980s. More important still was the widening gap between the vision and the fast changing realities of the Reagan/Thatcher era.

The 'masculine silhouette of the proletarian' that was supposed to guarantee the 'economically determined' 'historical inevitability' searched in vain for an original it might fit. In times of deregulation, 'outsourcing', 'subsidiarity', managerial disengagement, the phasing out of 'Fordist factories', the new 'flexibility' of employment patterns and working routines, and the gradual but relentless dismantling of the instruments of labour protection and self-defence, an expectation of a proletarian-led overhaul of social order and a proletarian-inspired cleansing of society of its evils must have strained the imagination beyond endurance. Most factory floors and office corridors became stages for tooth-and-nail, cut-throat competition between individuals struggling to catch the eye of the bosses and get a nod of approval – instead of being, as in the past, greenhouses of proletarian solidarity in the struggle for a better society. As Daniel Cohen, Sorbonne economist, found out, it was now the turn of each employee to show, by their own initiative, that they were better than the next person around, that they were bringing more profit to the shareholders of the company, and so would be worthy of keeping on when it came, as it was bound to, to the next round of 'rationalization' (read: more redundancies). Eye-opening studies by Fitoussi and Rosanvalon, by Boltanski and Chiapello amply and vividly confirmed that conclusion.

Pierre Bourdieu and Richard Sennett explained why the crumbling of previously stable settings and routines and the newly revealed frailty of even large and apparently solid firms does not favour a united, solidary stand and prevents individual troubles and anxieties from condensing into class conflict. As Boltanski and Chiapello put it, employees found themselves in a *cité par projets*, where the prospects of employment are confined to a single project currently under way. And among people living from one project to another, people whose life processes are sliced into a succession of short-lived projects, there is no time for diffuse discontents to condense into a bid for a better world... Such people would wish a *different today for each* rather than think seriously about a *better future for all*. Amidst the daily effort just to stay afloat, there is neither room nor time for a vision of the 'good society'.

All in all, factory halls and yards no longer seem secure enough as stocks in which to invest hopes of radical social change. The structures of capitalist enterprises and routines of hired labour, ever more friable and volatile, no longer seem to offer a common frame inside which variegated social deprivations and injustices can (let alone are bound to) blend, congeal and solidify into a programme for change; nor are they suitable as training grounds where marching columns can be formed and trained for imminent battle. There is no obvious home to be shared by social discontents. With the spectre of a proletarian-led revolution receding and dissipating, social grievances find themselves orphaned. They've lost the common ground on which common purposes can be negotiated and common strategies worked out. Each handicapped category is now on its own, abandoned to its own resources and its own ingenuity.

Many of such handicapped categories responded to the challenge. The 1980s was a decade of frantic craftsmanship; new banners were sewn and embroidered, manifestoes composed, placards designed and printed. With class no longer offering a secure linchpin for disparate and diffuse claims, social discontent dissolved into an indefinite number of group or categorial grievances, each seeking a social anchorage of its own. Gender, race and shared colonial pasts appeared to be the most effective and promising among them. Each one, though, had a struggle to emulate the integrating powers of class that had once pretended to the status of a 'meta-identity' on a par with that claimed by nationality in the nation-building era: to the status of the supra-identity, the most general, the

most voluminous and omnivorous of identities, the identity that would lend meaning to all other identities and
reduce them to the secondary, dependent status of 'special
cases' or 'exemplifications'. Each behaved as if it were
alone in the field, treating all competitors as false pretend-
ers. Each was oblivious, if not suspicious or openly hostile,
to similar exclusivity claims voiced and heard by others.

The 'unanticipated effect' of that was an accelerated
fragmentation of social dissent, a progressive disintegration of social conflict into a multitude of intergroup con-
frontations and a proliferation of battlegrounds. A
collateral casualty of the new recognition wars was the
idea of the 'good society' – an idea that could arouse and
hold the imagination only if credibility was added by the
presence of a supposed carrier, believed to be powerful and
determined enough to make the word flesh; but by then
such a carrier was nowhere in sight. The idea of a 'better
world', if it appeared at all, boiled down to the vindication
of current group-or category-related causes. It remained
indifferent to other deprivations and handicaps and
stopped far short of offering a universal, comprehensive
solution to human problems.

The carriers of new visions seemed, however, to over-
react to the discrediting of the preoccupation with economic injustice characteristic of class-related visions.
About the economic aspects and roots of human misery
– about the blatant and fast growing discrepancies in living
conditions, chances and prospects, rising poverty, the
wilting protection of human livelihoods, the jarring inequalities in wealth-and-income distribution – most new
visions kept petulantly silent. Richard Rorty's criticism of
the militants of the new 'social causes' is as pungent as it is
flawlessly on target: they prefer, Rorty says bluntly, 'not to
talk about money'.[14] Their (assumed) 'principal enemy is
a mind-set rather than a set of economic arrangements'. As

a result, the 'cultural left' to which they all belong 'is unable to engage in national politics'. To regain the political arena, it 'would have to talk more about money, even at the cost of talking less about stigma'.

I suspect that behind this bizarre blindness to economics lies the tendency described by Robert Reich as 'the secession of the successful': the renunciation of the duty which intellectuals who were social critics once believed they owed to the rest of their contemporaries, particularly those who were less privileged and happy than themselves. With that duty no longer acknowledged, their descendants may now focus on their own tender, touchy and sore spots, struggling to raise the respect and adulation they enjoy to the level of the economic heights they have already gained. They are, stubbornly, self-concerned and self-referential.

The war for social justice has therefore been short-changed into a plethora of battles for recognition. 'Recognition' may be the one thing that one or another sector of the successful misses most – the one thing that seems to be missing in the fast filling inventory of happiness factors. But for a large and rapidly growing part of humankind 'recognition' is a nebulous idea and will remain nebulous as long as money is shunned as a topic of conversation . . .

Pondering the failed prophecies of the past and glorious, though misdirected, hopes of the present, Rorty calls for people to sober up and awaken to the deep causes of human misery. 'We should ensure', he writes, that our children 'worry about the fact that the countries which industrialized first have a hundred times the wealth of those who have not yet industrialized. Our children need to learn, early on, to see the inequalities between their own fortunes and those of other children as neither the Will of God nor the necessary price for economic efficiency, but as an evitable tragedy.'[15]

Let me note that identification is also a powerful factor in stratification; one of its most divisive and sharply differentiating dimensions. At one pole of the emergent global hierarchy are those who can compose and decompose their identities more or less at will, drawing from the uncommonly large, planet-wide pool of offers. At the other pole are crowded those whose access to identity choice has been barred, people who are given no say in deciding their preferences and who in the end are burdened with identities enforced and imposed *by others*; identities which they themselves resent but are not allowed to shed and cannot manage to get rid of. Stereotyping, humiliating, dehumanizing, stigmatizing identities...

Most of us are suspended uneasily between those two poles, never sure how long our freedom to choose what we desire and renounce what we resent will last, or whether we will be able to keep the position we currently enjoy for as long as we would find it comfortable and desirable to hold it. Most of the time the joy of selecting an exciting identity is adulterated by fear. We know after all that if our efforts fail because of a dearth of resources or lack of determination, another, uninvited and unwanted, identity may be stuck over our chosen and self-assembled one. Max Frisch, writing from Switzerland – a country where individual (flexible) choices are reputedly presumed (and treated as) invalid unless stamped with popular (inflexible) approval – defined identity as the *rejection* of what others want you to be.

Wars of recognition, whether waged individually or collectively, are fought as a rule on two fronts, though troops and weapons are shifted between the frontlines depending on the position gained or allotted on the hierarchy of power. On one front, the chosen and preferred identity is advanced against, mostly, the obstinate leftovers of old, abandoned and resented identities, chosen or imposed in the past. On the other front, the pressures of other, contrived and enforced, identities (stereotypes, stigmas, labels) promoted by 'enemy forces' are fought back against and – if the battle is won – repulsed.

But even people who have been denied the right to assume the identity of their choice (a universally resented and feared predicament) have not yet landed in the lowermost regions of the power hierarchy; there is a lower space than low – a space underneath the bottom. Into this space fall (or, more correctly, are pushed) people who are denied the right to *claim* an identity as distinct from an ascribed and enforced classification; people whose petition won't be admitted and whose protests won't be heard even if they do petition for the annulment of the verdict. These are the people recently dubbed the 'underclass': exiled to the netherland out of the bounds of society – outside that assembly inside which identities (and so the right to a legitimate place in the totality) can be claimed, and once claimed are expected to be considered. If you have been assigned to the underclass (because you are a school dropout, or a single mother on welfare, or a current or former drug addict, or homeless, or a beggar, or a member of the other categories left out of the authoritatively endorsed list of those that are proper and admissible) any other identity you may covet and struggle to attain is a priori denied. The meaning of the 'underclass identity' is an *absence of identity*; the effacement or denial of individuality, of 'face' – that object of ethical duty and moral care. You are cast outside the social space in which identities are sought, chosen, constructed, evaluated, confirmed or refuted.

The 'underclass' is a motley collection of people who – as Giorgio Agamben would say – have had their 'bios' (that is, the life of a socially recognized subject) reduced to 'zoë' (purely animal life, with all its recognizably human offshoots trimmed or annulled). Another category that is

meeting the same fate are the refugees – the stateless, the
sans-papiers – the non-territorials in a world of territorially
grounded sovereignty. While sharing the predicament of
the underclass, they are, on top of all the other deprivations, denied the right to a physical presence within the
territory under sovereign rule except in specially designed
'non-places', labelled as refugee or asylum-seeker camps
to distinguish them from the space where the rest, the
'normal', the 'complete' people live and move.

The stake of the imperialism of the solid modern era was
the conquest of territory in order to magnify the volume of
labour subject to capitalist exploitation. Conquered lands
were taken over under the conquerors' administration, so
that the natives could be reprocessed into a sellable labour
force. That was (we could paraphrase Clausewitz's famed
adage) a continuation, a restaging on the global stage, of
the processes internally practised by each of the capitalist
countries of the West; and it resoundingly corroborated
and reaffirmed the Marx's selection of class as the principal determining factor of social identity. In the long run,
however, it has become salient that a most spectacular, and
perhaps even the most consequential, dimension of the
planetary-wide expansion of the West has been the slow
yet relentless globalization of the production of human
waste, or more precisely 'wasted humans' – humans no
longer necessary for the completion of the economic cycle
and thus impossible to accommodate within a social
framework resonant with the capitalist economy.

'Human waste' has been laid out from the start in every
land where such an economy was practised. As long as such
lands were confined to one part of the globe, however, an
effectively global 'waste disposal industry', in the form of
political and military imperialism, could neutralize the most
inflammatory potential of accumulating human waste. *Locally produced* problems sought, and found, a *global* solution.

Such solutions are no longer available: the expansion of the capitalist economy has finally caught up with the global extent of the political and military domination of the West and so the production of 'wasted humans' has become a planetary phenomenon. The 'problem of capitalism', the most blatant and potentially explosive malfunction of the capitalist economy, is shifting in its present planetary stage from exploitation to exclusion. It is exclusion, rather than the exploitation suggested a century and a half ago by Marx, that today underlies the most conspicuous cases of social polarization, of deepening inequality, and of rising volumes of human poverty, misery and humiliation.

We owe to Thomas Marshall the first speech where social rights of citizenship are seen as a frame, and inside this frame the clothes of collective identities are dismissed in favour of the citizen's clothes. Since then, identities have been coming out of the fog of the grand transformation, in order to inhabit modern time. How does this change take place, in your opinion?

This story has been told many times; and many times the dream of a republic that recognizes humanity in all its members and offers them all the entitlements due to human beings just because they are human beings – a republic that, at the same time as including members on the grounds of their humanity alone, is otherwise fully tolerant, perhaps even blind and oblivious, to their personal whims and idiosyncrasies (providing, of course, that they do not harm each other) – has been dreamt in every modern generation (Jürgen Habermas's 'constitutional patriotism' is its latest version). And no wonder. Such a republic seems to be the best imaginable solution to the most harrowing quandary of any form of human togetherness, namely how to live together with a minimum of conflict and strife and at the same time keep freedom of choice and self-assertion untainted. In brief: *how to achieve*

*unity in (in spite of?) difference and how to preserve difference
in (in spite of?) unity.*

Thomas Marshall's unique contribution was to general-
ize the sequence of political developments in Britain into a
'historical law', leading inextricably, everywhere, sooner or
later, from habeas corpus to political, and then to social
empowerment. At the threshold of the 'glorious thirty
years' of postwar reconstruction and 'social compact', the
British solution to the above mentioned quandary seemed
indeed inevitable and sooner or later irresistible. It was,
after all, the logical sequel to the core liberal creed, that in
order to become a fully fledged citizen of the republic one
needs to own the resources that leave time and energy free
from the struggle for bare survival. The bottom layer of
society, the proletarians, lacked such resources and were
unlikely to obtain them through their own industry and
savings – hence it was the republic itself which had to
guarantee the satisfaction of their basic needs so that
they could be integrated into the assembly of citizens.

In other words: it was hoped – believed – that once
personal security from oppression was achieved, people
would come together to settle their common affairs by
political action, and the result of the ever wider, in the
end universal, participation in politics would be collectively guaranteed survival – security from poverty, from the
bane of unemployment, from the inability to eke out daily
existence. To cut a long story short: once free, people
would become politically concerned and active, and
those people in turn would actively promote equity, justice, mutual care, brotherhood...

One should beware however of proclaiming a historical
sequence to be a manifestation of the 'iron laws of history'
and historical inevitability. One should beware even more
of foreclosing 'the logic of development' before that 'development' has run its course. There is no telling whether

a sequence of events is over, or at which point it will finish: human history stays stubbornly incomplete, and the human condition underdetermined. At the time Marshall wrote, the British variety of the 'welfare state' (better called, I think, the 'social state') did seem to be the culmination of the modern logic – a proper crowning of a tortuous but relentless and unstoppable historical drive, perhaps locally conceived but bound to be emulated – with modifications maybe, yet preserving the essentials – by all 'developed societies'.

In retrospect that conclusion seems, to say the least, premature. A mere thirty years after Lord Beveridge put the last touches on the blueprint for collective insurance against individual misfortune, and Marshall's rosy, optimistic vision of the resulting fullness of citizenship was put in writing, Kenneth Galbraith noted the advent of a 'contented majority' which used their newly acquired personal and political rights to vote their less shrewd or astute co-citizens out of a rising number of their social rights. Contrary to Beveridge's and Marshall's anticipations, the capacity of the social state to make the majority feel confident and contented has undermined its premises and ambitions instead of reinforcing them. Paradoxically, the self-confidence of the 'contented majority' which prompted them to withdraw support from the main principle of the social state – that of collective insurance against individual misfortune – was the outcome of the social state's astounding success. Having been lifted to the level of a genuine resourcefulness, to a position from which a wide assortment of opportunities beckoned to everyone with sufficient means at their disposal, that majority kicked away the ladder without which climbing to such a height would be hazardous or altogether impossible.

The process was self-propelling and self-accelerating. The shift in popular sentiment resulted in a progressive

shrinking of the protection which the no longer comprehensive social state was willing and able to offer. First, the
principle of collective insurance as the universal right of all
citizens was, through the practice of 'means testing', replaced with a promise of assistance aimed only at such
people who failed the test of resourcefulness and self-
sufficiency – and so, implicitly, the test of citizenship and
of 'full humanity'. Dependence on welfare handouts
became thereby not a citizenship right but a stigma
which self-respecting people would shun. Secondly,
following the rule that provision for poor people is poor
provision, welfare services in addition lost much of their
past attractiveness. Both factors added animus, speed and
volume to the escape of the 'contented majority' from the
'beyond left and right' alliance in support of the social
state. This led in turn to a further limitation and phasing
out of successive welfare provisions and an overall incap-
acitation of the welfare institution, starved of funds.

At the far end of the retreat from the social state lies the
desiccated, cracked and withered carapace of the 'republic',
bared of its most attractive trappings. Individuals struggling
with their life's challenges and told to seek private remedies
for socially produced problems cannot expect much assistance from the state. The reduced powers of the state do not
promise much – and guarantee even less. A rational person
would no longer trust the state to provide all that is needed
in case of unemployment, illness or old age, to assure
decent health care or proper education for children.
Above all, a rational person would not expect the state to
protect its subjects from blows falling seemingly at random
from the uncontrolled and poorly understood play of global
forces. And so there is a new, but already deeply rooted
feeling that even if one knew what a good society should be
like, an agency able and eager to fulfil such popular wishes
would not be found.

All in all, the meaning of 'citizenship' has been emptied of much of its past, genuine and postulated, contents, while the state-operated or state-endorsed institutions that sustained the credibility of that meaning have been progressively dismantled. The nation-state, as we've already noted, is no longer the natural depository for people's trust. Trust has been exiled from the home where it dwelled for the most part of modern history. It is floating now and drifting in search of alternative havens – but none of the alternatives on offer has so far managed to match the solidity and apparent 'naturalness' of the nation-state as a port of call.

There was a time when the human identity of a person was determined primarily by the productive role played in the social division of labour, when the state vouched (in its intentions and promises, even if not in practice) for the solidity and durability of that role, and when the state's subjects could call the state authorities to account in the event that they failed to deliver on their promises and to match up to their assumed responsibilities to the full satisfaction of their citizens. That unbroken chain of dependency and support could conceivably provide a foundation for something like Habermas's 'constitutional patriotism'. It seems, however, that an appeal to 'constitutional patriotism' as an effective remedy for the current troubles follows the habits of the Owl of Minerva's wings, known since Hegel's time to be spread at dusk, when the day is over... One explores the value of something in full only when it vanishes from view – goes missing or falls into disrepair.

Not much in the present state of affairs inspires hope for the chances of constitutional patriotism. For the centripetal pull of the state to override the centrifugal push of sectional, local and other particularistic, group-related and self-referential interests and concerns, the state must be able to offer something that cannot be gained as effectively at lower levels, and to tie together the strings of a safety net which otherwise would be left hanging loose. The time when the state was capable of such a feat, and trusted to do whatever was needed to see its task through, is now by and large over.

The state government is an address to which the denizens of an increasingly privatized and deregulated society are unlikely to send their complaints and stipulations. They have been told, repeatedly, to rely on their own wits, skills and industry, not to expect salvation from on high: to blame themselves, their own indolence or sloth, if they stumble or break their legs on their individual road to happiness. They may be excused for thinking that the powers-that-be have washed their hands of all responsibility for their fate (with the possible exception of locking up the paedophiles, cleaning the streets of prowlers, loiterers, beggars and other undesirables, and rounding up suspected terrorists before they become real ones). They feel abandoned to their own – sorely inadequate – resources, and their own – badly confused – initiative.

And what are the abandoned, desocialized, atomized, lonely individuals likely to dream of, and given a chance, do? Once the big harbours have been closed or stripped of the breakwaters that used to make them secure, the hapless sailors will be inclined to carve out and fence off their own small havens where they can anchor and deposit their bereaved, and fragile, identities. No longer trusting the public navigation network, they will jealously guard access to such private havens against all and any intruders.

For a sober mind the present spectacular rise of fundamentalisms holds no mystery. It is anything but puzzling or unexpected. Wounded by the experience of abandonment, men and women of our times suspect they are pawns in someone else's game, unprotected against the moves made by the big players, and easily disowned and earmarked for the rubbish heap whenever the big players find them no longer profitable. Whether in their consciousness or their subconscious, men and women of our times are haunted by the *spectre of exclusion*. They are aware – as Hauke Brunkhorst poignantly reminds us – that millions have already been excluded, and that for 'those who fall outside the functional system, be it in India, Brazil or Africa, or even as at present in many districts of New York or Paris, all others soon become inaccessible. Their voice will no longer be heard, often they are literally struck dumb.'[16] And so they fear being left alone with no loving heart and helping hand in sight, and badly miss the warmth, comfort and security of togetherness.

No wonder that for many people the fundamentalist promise of 'being born again' into a new warm and secure family-like home is a temptation they find hard to resist. They might have preferred something other than the fundamentalist therapy – a kind of security that does not require effacing their identity and surrendering their freedom to choose – but no such security is on offer. 'Constitutional patriotism' is not a realistic choice, whereas a fundamentalist community looks seductively simple. And so they will immerse themselves in its warmth right now, even if they expect to pay for the pleasure later. After all, have they not been brought up in a society of credit cards that take the waiting out of wanting?

With globalization, identity becomes a heated matter. All the landmarks are cancelled, biographies become jigsaw puzzles whose solutions are difficult and mutable. However, the problem is not the single pieces of this mosaic, but the way they fit in with each other. What is your opinion?

I am afraid that your allegory of jigsaw puzzles is only partly illuminating. Yes, you need to compose personal identity (identities?) in the way you compose a design out of jigsawed pieces, but you can compare biography only with a *defective* jigsaw puzzle, in which quite a few bits (and one will never know exactly how many) are missing. A jigsaw puzzle you buy from a shop is all in one box, with the final image already clearly printed on the box cover, and with a money-back guarantee that all the bits you need to replicate that image are inside the box and that no other image can be patched together using these bits; and so you can consult the image on the cover after every move to make sure that you are indeed on the right (the *only* correct) track to the known-in-advance destination and to see how much work remains to be done to reach it.

None of such comforts are available when you compose what is to be your identity. Yes, you have a lot of little pieces on the table which you hope to arrange into some meaningful whole – but the image which ought to emerge at the far end of your labour is not given in advance, so you cannot be sure whether you have all the bits you need to compose it, whether from those lying on the table you have selected the right ones, whether you've put them in the right places, and whether they have a place in the final design. We may say that the solving of jigsaw puzzles bought in a shop is *goal-oriented* : you start, so to speak, from the finishing line, from the final image known to you beforehand, and then pick up from the box one piece after another and try to fit them together. You are confident all along that eventually, with due effort, the right place for each piece and the right piece for each place will be found. The mutual fit of pieces and the completeness of their set are assured before you start. In the case of identity it is not like that at all: the whole labour is *means-oriented*. You do not start from the final image, but from a number of bits which you have already obtained or which seem to be worthy of having, and then you try to find out how you can order and reorder them to get some (how many?) pleasing pictures. You are *experimenting with what you have*. Your problem is not what you need in order to 'get there', to arrive at the point you want to reach, but what are the points that can be reached given the resources already in your possession, and which ones are worthy of your efforts to obtain them. We may say that the solving of jigsaw puzzles follows the logic of *instrumental* rationality (selecting the correct means to a given end); the construction of identity, on the other hand, is guided by the logic of *goal* rationality (finding out how attractive the ends are that can be achieved with the given means). The job of an identity-constructor is, as Claude Lévi-Strauss would say, that of a *bricoleur*, conjuring up all sorts of things out of the material at hand....

It was not always like that. Once modernity replaced premodern *estates* (which determined identity by birth and hence provided few if any occasions for the question of 'who am I?' to arise) with *classes*, identities became tasks which individuals had to perform, as you rightly suggest, through their biographies. As Jean-Paul Sartre memorably put it then, to be a bourgeois it is not enough to be born a bourgeois – one needs to live one's whole life as a bourgeois! When it comes to class membership, one needs to *prove* by one's deeds, by one's 'whole life' – not just by brandishing a birth certificate – that one indeed belongs to the class one claims to belong to. By failing to supply such convincing proof, one can lose class assignment, become *déclassé*.

For the greater part of the modern era it was crystal clear what such proof should consist of. Each class had, we may say, its career tracks, its trajectory unambiguously laid out, signposted all along the way and punctuated with milestones permitting the wanderers to monitor their progress. There was little if any doubt as to the shape of life needing to be lived in order to be, say, a bourgeois – and to be recognized as such. Above all, that shape seemed to be carved out once and for all. One could follow the trajectory step by step, acquiring successive class insignia in their proper, 'natural' order, without worrying that the signposts might be moved or turned round the other way before the journey was completed.

Setting 'identity' as a task and the goal of lifelong labour was, as compared to the premodern ascription to estates, an act of liberation; a liberation from the inertia of traditional ways, from immutable authorities, from preordained routines and unquestionable truths. But, as Alain Peyrefitte found in his thorough historical study,[17] that new, unprecedented freedom of self-identification that followed the decomposition of the estate system arrived together with a new and unprecedented self-confidence and trust in others, as well as in the merits of the company of others which was given the name of 'society': in its collective wisdom, the reliability of its instructions, the durability of its institutions. To dare and take risks, to have the courage that choice-making requires, such a triple confidence (in oneself, in others, in society) is needed. One needs to believe that trust in *socially made* choices is well placed and that the future appears certain; one needs society as an umpire, not as another player who keeps cards close to his chest and is fond of surprising you . . .

The most perceptive observers of modern life noted quite early, already in the nineteenth century, that the trust in question was not as solidly grounded as the 'official version' – struggling to become the dominant, perhaps the only creed – insinuated. One of these acute observers was Robert Musil, who at the very beginning of the last century noted that 'society no longer functions properly', at the time when individuals had 'reached the heights of sophistication'.[18] The shifting of responsibilities for choice onto individual shoulders, the dismantling of signposts and the removing of milestones, topped up by a growing indifference of the powers-on-high to the nature of the choices made and to their feasibility, were two trends present in the 'challenge of self-identification' from the start. In the course of time the two trends, closely intertwined and mutually invigorating, gathered force – even if they were frowned on, bewailed and censured as worrying, even pathological, developments.

The principal moving force behind that process has all along been the accelerating 'liquefaction' of social frameworks and institutions. We are now passing from the 'solid' to the 'fluid' phase of modernity; and 'fluids' are so called because they cannot keep their shape for long, and unless they are poured into a tight container they keep changing shape under the influence of even the slightest of forces. In a fluid setting, there is no knowing whether to expect a flood or a drought – it is better to be ready for both eventualities. Frames, when (if) they are available, should not be expected to last for long. They will not be able to withstand all that leaking, seeping, trickling, spilling – sooner rather than later they will drench, soften, contort and decompose. Today's respected authorities will be ridiculed, snubbed or despised tomorrow, celebrities will be forgotten, trend-setting idols will be remembered only in TV quizzes, cherished novelties will be dumped on rubbish tips, eternal causes will be elbowed out by other causes similarly claiming eternity (though, having repeatedly singed their fingers, people will not believe their claims any longer), indestructible powers will fade and dissipate, mighty political or economic establishments will be swallowed up by other even mightier ones, or just vanish, the foolproof stocks will turn into the fool's stocks, promising lifelong careers will be found to be blind alleys. All that feels like inhabiting an Escher universe, where no one, at no point, can tell the difference between a way uphill and a descending slope.

'Society' is no longer believed to be a stern and uncom-
promising, occasionally severe and merciless, yet hopefully
a fair, principled arbiter of human trials and errors. It
reminds one rather of a particularly shrewd, cunning and
duplicitous poker-faced player in the game of life, cheating
if given a chance, flouting rules whenever possible; in
short, a pastmaster of underhand tricks that as a rule
catch all or most other players unprepared. Its power no
longer lies in a straightforward coercion: society gives no
commands on how to live – and were it to give commands,
it would care little whether or not they were obeyed.
'Society' wants from you nothing but to stay in the game
and have enough tokens left on the table to go on
playing.

The might of society and its power over individuals now
rests instead on its being 'unpinpointable', on its evasive-
ness, versatility and volatility, the perplexing unpredict-
ability of its moves, the Houdini-like dexterity with which
it escapes from the toughest of cages and the deftness with
which it defies expectations and goes back on its promises,
whether outspoken or cleverly insinuated. The right strategy to deal with such an erratic and evasive player it to beat
him at his own game . . .

Don Juan (as portrayed by Molière, Mozart or Kierkegaard) may be named as an inventor and pioneer of that
strategy. By Molière's Don Juan's own admission, the
delight of love consists in incessant change. The secret of
Mozart's Don Giovanni's conquests, in Kierkegaard's
opinion, was his knack for finishing quickly and starting
from a new beginning; Don Giovanni was in a state of
perpetual self-creation. In Ortega y Gasset's view, Don
Juan/Don Giovanni was a true embodiment of the vitality
of spontaneous living and that made him the foremost
manifestation of the basic uneasiness, the concerns and
anxieties of modern humans. All that prompted Michel

Serres (in 'The apparition of Hermes', in his *Hermes*) to nominate Don Juan as the first hero of modernity. Taking a hint from Camus (who observed that a seducer in the Don Juan style dislikes looking at portraits), Beata Frydryczak, a perceptive philosopher of culture, has noted that this 'hero of modernity' could not be a collector, since what counted for him was just the 'here and now', the fleeting moment. If he did collect something – his collectables were sensations, excitements, *Erlebnisse*.[19] And sensations are by their nature as frail and short-lived, as volatile as the situations that triggered them. The strategy of *carpe diem* is a response to a world emptied of values pretending to be lasting.

What (I believe) follows is that your suggestion that the problem is 'the way they' (the various bits of which the supposedly cohesive identity is composed) 'fit in with each other' is revealing but incorrect. Fitting bits and pieces together into a consistent and cohesive totality called 'identity' does not seem to be the main worry of our contemporaries, who have been cast forcibly and irredeemably into a Don Juan-style predicament and are thereby forced to adopt Don Juan's strategy. Perhaps this is not their worry at all. A *cohesive*, firmly riveted and solidly constructed identity would be a burden, a constraint, a limitation on the freedom to choose. It would portend an incapacity to unlock the door when the next opportunity knocks. To cut a long story short, it would be a recipe for *inflexibility* – that is for a condition that keeps being decried, ridiculed or condemned by virtually all genuine or putative authorities of the day – the mass media, learned experts in human problems, and political leaders alike – for opposing the correct and prudent, success-promising attitude to life and so being a condition that it is almost unanimously recommended to be wary of and scrupulously avoided.

For a great majority of the denizens of a liquid modern world, such attitudes as a care for cohesion, sticking to the rules, abiding by precedents and staying loyal to the logic of continuity rather than floating on the wave of changeable and short-lived opportunities are not promising options. If they are adopted by some other people (seldom willingly, to be sure!), they are promptly singled out as symptoms of social deprivation and a stigma of an unsuccessful life, of defeat, of lesser value, of social inferiority. In public awareness, they tend to be associated with a life in prison or in an urban ghetto, with assignment to the detested and abhorred 'underclass', or with confinement in the camps of stateless refugees...

Projects to which one would swear lifelong loyalty once they were selected and embraced (Jean Paul Sartre only half a century ago recommended *projets de la vie*) have a bad press and have lost their attraction. Most people, if pressed, would describe them as counterproductive and surely not a kind of choice they would gladly make. Going on and on *fitting* bits together – yes, there is nothing else you can do. But to *fit* them together, to find *the best* fit that puts an end to the game of fitting? No, thank you, this is something one could do better without.

Towards the end of a life spent in endless efforts to compose the perfect harmony of pure colours and geometrically clean forms (perfection being a state that cannot be improved, so barring all further change), Piet Mondrian, the great visual poet of solid modernity, painted 'Victory boogie-woogie': a furious, tumultuous cacophony of formless shapes and jarring red, orange, pink, green and blue hues...

One of the consequences of these transformations is the re-emerging of nationalism. Thus, if biographies become full of jigsaw pieces, what we have is the paradox that the word 'community' (Gemeinschaft) forcefully re-enters the discussion. Is it a paradox? Or, on the other hand, are these phenomena complementary?

Again, I am not sure whether your diagnosis is a hundred per cent correct. It is true that the various movements seeking community/recognition that are cropping up these days in lands where the 'national question' seemed to have been solved a hundred or so years ago (and for a long time to come, perhaps finally and forever) tend to be commonly interpreted as the 're-emerging of nationalism'. When all hell broke out in the Balkans after the collapse of the Yugoslav state union, Tom Nairn summarized the dominant view of the events as a resurfacing of a dark, archaic, atavistic, irrational force, dormant until recently and thought to be deceased, but apparently never really, irrevocably dead – and now once more 'compelling peoples to place blood before reasonable progress and individual rights'.[20] The question which this and similar diagnoses suggested and prompted to be asked was 'why did the undead rise?' It was the kind of question that films about vampires and zombies keep asking; a question as misleading and fanciful as the idea itself of 'rising from the undead' or a miraculous preservation of primeval hatreds in a freezer of the collective unconscious. Though it is easy to understand why an old name has been used to denote novel and not fully understood phenomena, resorting to tried and tested conceptual fishing nets whenever bizarre sea creatures appear, never seen before, is, after all, a common and time-honoured habit. But we should heed Derrida's warning and be aware that we can use old concepts, inevitably filled with outdated meanings, only 'under erasure'.

There are two obvious reasons for this new crop of claims to autonomy or independence, wrongly described as a 'resurgence of nationalism' or a resurrection/revival of nations. One reason is an earnest and desperate, even if misguided, attempt to find protection from the globalizing winds that are sometimes freezing, sometimes scorching, a protection which the crumbling walls of the nation-state no longer provide. Another is a rethinking of the traditional compact between nation and state, only to be expected at a time when the weakening states have fewer and fewer benefits to offer in exchange for the loyalty demanded in the name of national solidarity. As you can see, both reasons point to the *erosion of state sovereignty* as the main factor. The movements under discussion manifest the wish to readjust the received strategy of the collective pursuit of interests, seeking or creating new stakes and new actors in the power game. We may (and should) frown on the separatist zeal of such movements, we may condemn the tribal hatreds they sow and bewail the bitter fruits of the sowing – but we can hardly charge them with irrationality or dismiss them as simply an atavistic hiccup. If we do that, we risk mistaking what needs to be explained for the explanation.

The Scots 'rediscovered' their nationhood complete with patriotic fervour when the government in London began to pocket the profits from selling licences to drill for oil off the Scottish seashore (that born-again nationalism started losing many a newly recruited patriot once the bottom began to show below the North Sea oilrigs). As the grip of the government in Rome began to weaken, and little gain from loyalty to the shared state was on the cards, the people of the affluent north of Italy asked why the poor, hapless and shiftless Calabrians or Sicilians should be bailed out of their misery year after year at their, the Northerners', expense – and so the questioning of the common Italian national identity promptly followed.

At the first signs of the Yugoslav state's imminent demise, the businesslike and well-off Slovenians wondered why their wealth should go on being siphoned off to the less fortunate parts of the Slav alliance, landing first in the hands of the Belgrade bureaucrats. Let us also recall that it was the German Chancellor Helmut Kohl who *first* voiced the opinion that Slovenia deserved an independent state *because it was ethnically homogeneous* – it could be a spark that made the Balkan powder keg of ethnicities, languages, religions and alphabets explode into a frenzy of ethnic cleansing.

The tragedy that followed is well known. But the alleged 'atavistic drives' did not *spring out* of the dark depths of the unconscious, where they had hibernated since time immemorial waiting for the moment of awakening to arrive. They had to be laboriously *construed* – by cunningly setting a neighbour against a neighbour, one member of kin against another, and by transforming everyone earmarked for membership of the projected community into an active accomplice of crime or an accessory after the fact. Killing next-door neighbours, rape, bestiality, murder of the defenceless – breaking one by one all the most sacred taboos, and breaking them in public view, in full limelight – was in fact an act of community *creation*: conjuring up a community tied together by the memory of the *original misdeed*; a community that could be reasonably sure of its survival thanks to becoming the only shield protecting the perpetrators from being declared criminals instead of heroes, from being brought to trial and punished. But why did people obey those calls to arms in the first place? Why did neighbours turn against neighbours?

The swift and spectacular collapse of the state that serviced the frame in which neighbourly intercourse could be routinely conducted was undoubtedly a traumatic experience, a good reason to fear for one's security. Among the ruins of the state-supervised framework, the weeds of anxiety sprang and ran wild. A genuine 'social crisis' followed, and, as René Girard explains, in a state of social crisis 'people inevitably blame either society as a whole, which costs them nothing, or other people who seem particularly harmful for easily identifiable reasons.' In a state of social crisis, frightened individuals huddle together and become a crowd – and 'the crowd by definition seeks action but cannot affect natural causes [of crisis]. It therefore looks for an accessible cause that will appease its appetite for violence.' The rest is rather confusing, but easy to accomplish and to understand: 'In order to blame victims for the loss of distinctions resulting from the crisis, they are accused of crimes that eliminate distinctions. But in actuality they are identified as victims for persecution because they bear the signs of victims.'[21]

When the familiar world falls to pieces, one of the most off-putting and disquieting effects is the pile of debris hiding the borders and the falling junk and scraps breaking the signposts. The would-be victims are not feared and hated for being different – but for being *not different enough*, mixing too easily into the crowd. Violence is needed to make them spectacularly, unmistakably, blatantly different. Then by destroying them one could hopefully eliminate the polluting agent that blurred the distinctions and thereby recreate an orderly world in which everyone knows who they are and identities are no longer frail, uncertain and precarious. So, true to the modern pattern, all destruction here is a *creative* destruction: a holy war of order against chaos, an action with purpose, an order-building labour...

Let there be no mistake: social crisis caused by the loss of the conventional means of effective collective protection is not a Balkan speciality. With different degrees of sharpness and condensation, it is experienced throughout our fast globalizing planet. Its consequences in the Balkans might have been uncharacteristically extreme, but similar mechanisms are in operation elsewhere. Things may not go as far as in the Balkans and the drama may be muted, sometimes even inaudible, but similar desires and compulsive urges spur people into action whenever the dreadfully disturbing effects of social crisis are felt.

The most widely and keenly coveted goal is the digging of deep, possibly impassable trenches between the 'inside' of a territorial or categorial locality and the 'outside'. Outside: tempests, hurricanes, frosty gales, ambushes along the road and dangers all around. Inside: cosiness, warmth, *chez soi*, security, safety. Since to make the whole planet secure (so that we no longer need to separate ourselves from the inhospitable 'outside') we lack (or at least believe that we lack) adequate tools and raw materials, let's carve out, fence off and fortify a plot distinctly ours and no one else's, a plot inside which we can feel ourselves to be the only and uncontested masters. The state can no longer claim enough power to protect its territory and its residents. So the task that has been abandoned and dropped by the state lies on the ground, waiting for someone to pick it up. What follows is not, contrary to widespread opinion, a rebirth or even a posthumous vengeance of nationalism – it is a desperate, though vain, search for *substitute local solutions to globally generated troubles*, in a situation in which one can no longer count for help in this matter on the conventional state-run agencies.

The distinction between the republican artifice of citizenship's consensus and 'natural' insiderness/membership/belonging goes as far back as the *querelle* in the eighteenth and early nineteenth centuries between French philosophers of the Enlightenment and German Romantics (Herder, Fichte), the theorists of *Volk* and *Volkgeist* that precede and override all artificial identities and distinctions which may be legislated on to human togetherness. Those two concepts of nationhood were given canonical form in Friedrich Meinecke's opposition of

Staatnation and *Kulturnation* (1907). Geneviève Zubrzycki
summarized her survey of definitions current in contemporary political as well as social-scientific debates by opposing the 'civic' and the 'ethnic' models/interpretations of
the nationhood phenomenon.

> According to the civic model of nationhood, national
> identity is purely political; it is nothing but the individual's
> choice to belong to a community based on the associa-
> tion of like-minded individuals. The ethnic version on
> the contrary maintains that national identity is purely
> cultural. Identity is given at birth; it imposes itself on the
> individual.[22]

The opposition is, in the last account, between belonging
by *primordial assignment* or by *choice*. In practical terms,
between a *brute fact* that precedes the thoughts and choices
of individual humans, a fact that, after the pattern of
genetically inherited and determined traits of the human
body, can be belied, pasted over or otherwise concealed
but never realistically wished away or 'undone', and an
assembly that, like a club or voluntary association, can be
joined and left at will, and whose shape, character and
procedure are constantly open to its members' deliber-
ation and renegotiation.

But let me note that the word 'cultural' by which the
first of the two models is today commonly described is a
misnomer dictated by the current standards of 'political
correctness'. After all, 'culture' entered our vocabulary
two centuries ago carrying a precisely opposite meaning:
as the antonym of 'nature', denoting such human
features as, in stark opposition to the obstinate facts of
nature, are products, sediments or side-effects of *human
choices*. Human-made, they can in principle be human
unmade.

Let me note also that the Romantic concept originated in a 'nation without a state', German-speaking central Europe divided into countless and mostly minute political units, while the Enlightenment-republican notion was conceived in a 'state without a nation', a territory under increasingly centralized dynastic administration struggling to introduce a measure of coherence into a conglomerate of ethnicities, dialects and 'local cultures' – customs, beliefs, routines, mythologies, calendars. The two notions do not stand for two alternative types of nationhood, but for two successive glosses over the nature of human togetherness in various stages of cohabitation, engagement, marriage and divorce between nation and state. Each gloss is resonant with a somewhat different political task and practice. One serves better the needs of the struggle for statehood, while the other services the 'nation-building' efforts of the political state.

In view of the current separation and the looming divorce between state and nation, with the political state abandoning its assimilatory ambitions, declaring neutrality towards cultural choices and washing its hands of the increasingly 'multicultural' character of the society it administers, it is no wonder that so-called 'cultural' visions of identity are coming back into fashion among the groups that seek stable and secure havens amidst the tides of uncertain change.

To insecure people, perplexed, confused and frightened by the instability and contingency of the world they inhabit, 'community' appears to be a tempting alternative. It is a sweet dream, a vision of heaven: of tranquillity, bodily safety and spiritual peace. For people tussling in the tight net of constraints, prescriptions and proscriptions, people struggling for freedom of choice and self-assertion, the self-same community demanding unswerving loyalty and closely guarding its entries and exits is, on the contrary, a

nightmare: a vision of hell or prison. The point is that we
are all, intermittently or simultaneously, overwhelmed
with 'too much responsibility' and desirous of 'more freedom' that cannot but add further to our responsibilities.
For most of us, therefore, 'community' is a Janus-faced,
utterly ambiguous phenomenon, loved or hated, loved *and*
hated, attractive or repelling, attractive *and* repelling. One
of the most haunting, mind-boggling and nerve-wracking
among the many ambivalent choices we, the denizens of
the liquid modern world, face daily.

In this reshuffling, even the basic forms of social relationship go through a
mutation. From amorous relationships to religion everything becomes unstable,
liquid. But how do amorous relationships change?

You've put your finger here on another formidable ambivalence of our liquid modern times. Interpersonal relationships with all their accompaniments – love, partnerships,
commitments, mutually recognized rights and duties – are
simultaneously objects of attraction and apprehension,
desire and fear; sites of two-mindedness and hesitation,
soul-searching, anxiety. As I have suggested elsewhere (in
Liquid Love), after Robert Musil's Man without Qualities
came our own, liquid modern 'Man without Bonds'. Most
of us, most of the time, are in two minds about that novelty
of 'bond-free living' – of relationships 'with no strings
attached'. We covet and fear them at the same time. We
wouldn't go back, but we feel ill at ease where we are now.
We are unsure how to make the relationships we desire;
worse still, we are not sure what kind of relationships we
desire . . .

I believe that Erich Fromm grasped the dilemma in its
essence when he observed that 'satisfaction in individual
love cannot be attained . . . without true humility, courage,

faith and discipline', but added right away, with sadness, that in 'a culture in which these qualities are rare, the attainment of the capacity to love must remain a rare achievement'.[23] To love means being determined to share and blend two biographies, each carrying a different load of experiences and memories and each running its own course; it means by the same token an agreement to the future and so to a *great unknown*. In other words, as Lucan observed two millennia ago and Francis Bacon repeated many centuries after, it means giving hostages to fate. It also means making oneself dependent on another person endowed with a similar freedom to choose and the will to follow that choice – and so a person full of surprises, unpredictable.

My desire for loving and being loved can be only fulfilled if it is supported by a genuine readiness to see it 'through thick and thin', to compromise my own freedom if need be so that the freedom of the beloved is not violated. In Plato's *Symposium*, Diotima of Mantinea (that is 'prophetess Fearthelord of Prophetville') pointed out to Socrates, with the latter's wholehearted agreement, that 'love is not for the beautiful, as you think.' 'It is for begetting and birth in the beautiful.' To love is to desire 'to beget and procreate' and so the lover 'seeks and goes about to find the beautiful thing in which he can beget'. In other words, it is not in craving after ready-made, complete and finished things that love finds its meaning – but in the urge to participate in, and contribute to, the becoming of such things. Love is akin to transcendence; it is but another name for creative drive and as such it is fraught with risks, as are all the creative processes, never sure where they are going to end.

We end up with a paradox. We started guided by a hope for a solution – only to find new problems. We sought love to find succour, confidence, security – but the indefinitely

long, perhaps interminable labours of love gestate con-
frontations, uncertainty, insecurities of their own. In
love, there are no quick fixes, no once-and-for-ever solutions, no assurance of perpetual and full satisfaction, no
money-back guarantee in case full satisfaction is not instant and unalloyed. All those paid-for anti-risk devices
that our consumer society has taught us to expect are
absent in love. But pampered by the promises lavished
on us by shopkeepers, we've lost the skills needed to face
the risks and to tackle them on our own. And so we are
inclined to beat love relationships flat into the 'consumerist' mode, the only one with which we feel secure and
comfortable.

The 'consumerist mode' demands that satisfaction
needs to be, must be, better be, instant, while the sole
value, the only 'use', of objects is their capacity to give
satisfaction. Once satisfaction stops (because of the
objects' wear and tear, because of their excessive, increasingly dull familiarity, or because other, less familiar, untested and thus more exciting replacements are on offer)
there is no reason to clutter the house with those useless
objects.

One of the perennially favourite Christmas gifts to
English children is a dog (usually a puppy). On the present-day plight of that habit, Andrew Morton recently
commented that dogs, known to be eminently adaptable
to human environments and human routines, should 'start
reducing their life expectancy from approximately 15 years
to something more in tune with modern attention spans:
say about three months' (this is the average time that
passes before the joyfully welcome dogs are thrown out
of the house). A high percentage of the people chasing
their pets out of their houses 'have been getting rid of
them in order to make way for another, more fashionable
dog'.[24]

As with pet animals, so with pet humans. Barbara Ellen, an *Observer Magazine* columnist, writes of 'dumping the partner' as of a normal event. 'We are always being told that death is an important part of life. In the same way, isn't the break-up an important part of the relationship?'[25] Break-up, it seems, is now viewed as an event as 'natural' as death is to life – since relationships, once coveted as the gangway into eternity of mortal humans, have themselves turned fissiparous and mortal; plagued, indeed, with a life expectation many times shorter than that of the individuals who put them together only to break them up again. Another witty British columnist suggested that marrying is like 'embarking on a sea voyage on a raft made of blotting paper'.

Animals or humans, pets or partners – does it matter? They are all here for the same purpose: to satisfy (at least this is what we keep them for). If they don't, they have no purpose at all and so no reason to be here. Anthony Giddens famously suggested that the old romantic idea of love as an exclusive partnership 'till death us do part' has been replaced, in the course of individual liberation, by 'confluent love' – a relationship that lasts only as long as, and not a moment longer than, the satisfaction it brings to both partners. In the case of relationships, you want the 'permit to go in' to come together with a 'permit to go out' the moment you see no more reason to stay.

Giddens views that change in the nature of relationships as liberating: partners are now free to go away to seek satisfaction elsewhere if they fail to draw it, or stop drawing it, from the current relationship. What he does not mention, though, is that because the beginning of a relationship requires the consent of two, while a decision of just one partner is sufficient for its termination, all partnerships are doomed to be permanently shot with anxiety: what if the other person gets bored before I do? Another consequence that Giddens does not notice is that the availability of an easy way out is itself a formidable obstacle to the fulfilment of love. It makes the kind of long-term effort such fulfilment would require much less probable, likely to be abandoned well before a gratifying conclusion can be reached, rejected as 'poor value for money', or resented because of a price one sees no reason to pay in view of the apparently cheaper substitutes available on the market.

Three months is very nearly the maximum time during which the young trainees of consumer society are able first to enjoy, and then to tolerate the company of their pets. They are likely to carry that early acquired habit into later life, when humans replace the dogs as love objects. Morton blames the shortening of the 'attention span'. One could, however, seek the causes elsewhere. If our ancestors were shaped and trained by their societies as producers first and foremost, we are increasingly shaped and trained as consumers first, and all the rest after. Attributes considered to be assets in a producer (the acquisition and retention of habits, loyalty to established customs, tolerance of routine and repetitive behaviour patterns, readiness to delay gratification, fixity of needs) turn into the most awesome vices in the case of a consumer. Were they to stay or become common, they would sound the death-knell of the consumer-focused economy.

The education of a consumer is not a one-off campaign or a once-and-for-all achievement. It starts early, but it fills the rest of life; the cultivation of consumer skills is perhaps the sole successful case of that 'continuing education' which the theorists and practitioners of education currently advocate. The institutions of 'lifelong consumer education' are countless and ubiquitous – starting from the daily flood of TV, newspaper and wall and billboard commercials, through the oodles of glossy 'thematic' magazines vying to publicize the lifestyles of trend-setting celebrities, the grand masters of the consumerist arts, and up to the vociferous experts/counsellors offering state-of-the-art, thoroughly researched and laboratory-proved recipes for spotting and resolving 'life problems'.

Let us stop for a moment at those experts who specialize in writing recipes for human relations, and particularly for love partnerships. 'Semi-detached couples' are to be praised as 'relationship revolutionaries who have burst the suffocating couple bubble', writes one of them in a highly respected and widely read magazine. Another expert/counsellor informs readers that 'when committing yourself, however half-heartedly, remember that you are likely to be closing the door on other romantic possibilities which may be more satisfying and fulfilling.' Another expert suggests that relationships, like cars, must periodically go through a test of road-worthiness and be withdrawn from use in the event that the results are negative. Yet another expert sounds even blunter: 'Promises of commitment are meaningless in the long term... Like other investments, they wax and wane.' And so, if you wish 'to relate', keep your distance; if you want fulfilment from your togetherness, do not make or demand commitments. Keep all doors open at all times.

All in all, what we would learn from the relationship experts is that commitment, and particularly a long-term commitment, is a trap that those seeking 'to relate' should avoid more than any other danger. The span of human attention has shrunk – but yet more seminal is the shrinking of the timespan of forecasting and planning. The future has always been uncertain, but its capriciousness and volatility have never felt so intractable as they do in the liquid modern world of 'flexible' labour, frail human bonds, fluid moods, floating threats and an unstoppable cavalcade of chameleon-like dangers. Never has it been felt so strongly that the future is, as Emmanuel Levinas has suggested, 'the absolute other' – inscrutable, impermeable, unknowable, and in the end beyond human control.

In a world where disengagement is practised as a common strategy of the power struggle and self-assertion, there are few if any firm points in life that can be safely predicted to last. The 'present' does not therefore bind the 'future', and there is nothing in the present that allows us to guess, let alone to visualize, the shape of things to come. Long-term thinking and, even more, long-term commitments and obligations indeed appear 'meaningless'. Worse still, they seem counterproductive, downright dangerous, a foolish step to take, ballast that needs to be thrown overboard and would have been better not taken on board in the first place.

All this is worrying, indeed frightening news. The blows strike right into the heart of the human mode of being-in-the-world. After all, the hard core of identity – the answer to the question 'Who am I?' and even more importantly the continuing credibility of whatever answer might have been given to that question – cannot be formed unless in reference to the bonds connecting the self to other people and the assumption that such bonds are reliable and stable over time. We need relationships, and we need relationships in which we count for something, relationships to which we can refer in order to define ourselves. But because of the long-term commitments which they notoriously inspire or inadvertently spawn, relationships may be, in a liquid modern environment, fraught with dangers. We need them nonetheless, we need them badly, and not only because of moral concern for the well-being of others, but also for our own sake, for the sake of the cohesion and logic of our own being. When it comes to entering and staying in a relationship, *fear and desire fight to get the better of each other.* We earnestly struggle for the security that only a committed relationship (and yes, committed for the long term!) may bring – and yet we fear a victory no less than defeat. Our attitudes to human bonds tend to be painfully ambivalent, and the chances of resolving that ambivalence are nowadays slim.

There is no easy way out from this predicament, and certainly no feasible radical cure for the torments of ambivalence. And so there is a rabid and furious search for second-best solutions, half-solutions, temporary solutions, palliatives, placebos. Everything will do that can push the gnawing doubts and unanswerable questions aside, postpone the moment of reckoning and truth – and so allow us to keep on the move even if the destination is, to say the least, wrapped in fog.

If the quality cannot be trusted, perhaps the quantity may bring salvation? If each relationship is fragile, perhaps the expedient of multiplying and piling relationships up will make the ground feel less treacherous? Thank God you *can* pile them up – precisely because they are, each one of them, brittle and disposable! And so we seek rescue in 'networks', whose advantage over hard-and-fast bonds is that they make connecting and disconnecting equally easy (as a twenty-six-year-old man from Bath recently explained, he prefers 'internet dating' to 'singles bars' because if something goes wrong 'it is enough to press "delete"'; in a face-to-face encounter you cannot dump the unwelcome partner so effortlessly). And we use our mobile telephones to chat and message so we can constantly feel the comfort of 'being in touch' without the discomforts which actual 'touching' may hold in store. We replace the few depth *relationships* with a mass of thin and shallow *contacts*.

I guess that the inventors and merchandisers of 'visual mobiles', designed to transmit images in addition to voices and written messages, have miscalculated: they won't find a mass market for their gadgets. I guess that the necessity to look the partner of the 'virtual contact' in the eye, to enter the state of *visual* (even if virtual) proximity, will deprive the mobile chatting of the main advantage for which it was so enthusiastically embraced by the millions who crave to 'keep in touch' while keeping their distance at the same time . . .

What those millions crave is best served by 'messaging', which eliminates simultaneity and continuity from the exchange, thereby stopping short of becoming a genuine, and so risky, dialogue. Audial contact comes second. Audial contact is a dialogue, but happily free from eye contact, that illusion of closeness that carries all the dangers of inadvertently betraying (by gestures, mimicry, eye expression) what the chatters would rather keep out of the 'relationship'. Such reduced, 'sanitized' relating fits well with the rest of it – the liquid world of fluid identities, the world in which finishing quickly, moving on and starting anew is the name of the game, the world of commodities spawning and brandishing ever new tempting desires in order to smother and forget the desires of yore.

Freedom to move on is the prize, but one option we are not free to choose is to stop moving. As Ralph Waldo Emerson already warned a long time ago, if you skate on thin ice your salvation is in speed.

And how does the attitude towards the sacred change?

Not an easy question to answer. To start with, 'the sacred' is a notoriously vague and hotly contested concept, and it is awfully difficult to be sure, and even more to agree, about what we are talking about. Some writers go as far as to suggest that the sacred is confined to what goes on inside a church or its equivalent; some other writers suggest that the Sunday car-washing or family trip to a shopping mall is the present-day incarnation of the sacred . . .

But even if we dismiss and forget such extreme and rather silly suggestions (themselves, in my view, manifestations of the 'crisis of the sacred') and accept that what you are asking about are phenomena of the kind that Rudolph Otto tried to grasp in the idea of 'tremendous' or Immanuel Kant in the concept of 'sublime', the task does not become much easier. Perhaps it will help to make clearer what such phenomena consist of?

When trying to unravel the mystery of earthly, human power, Mikhail Bakhtin, one of the greatest Russian philosophers of the past century, began from the description of 'cosmic fear' – a *human*, all-too-human emotion aroused by the unearthly, *inhuman* magnificence of the universe; in his view the kind of fear that serves man-made power as its foundation, prototype and inspiration.[26] *Cosmic* fear is, in Bakhtin's words, the trepidation felt 'in the face of the immeasurably great and immeasurably powerful: in the face of the starry heavens, the material mass of the mountains, the sea, and the fear of cosmic upheavals and elemental disasters'. At the core of 'cosmic fear' lies, let us note, the nonentity of the frightened, wan and transient human being faced with the enormity of the everlasting universe; the sheer weakness, incapacity for resistance, *vulnerability* of the frail and soft human body that the sight of the 'starry heavens' or 'the material mass of the mountains' reveals; but also the realization that it is not in the power of humans to grasp, comprehend, mentally assimilate that awesome might which manifests itself in the sheer grandiosity of the universe. Pascal described that feeling, and its source, flawlessly:

> When I consider the brief span of my life absorbed into the eternity which comes before and after . . . the small space I

occupy and which I see swallowed up in the infinite im-
mensity of spaces of which I know nothing and which
knows nothing of me, I take fright and am amazed to see
myself here rather than there, now rather than then.[27]

That universe escapes all understanding. Its intentions are
unknown, its 'next steps' are unpredictable. If there is a
preconceived plan or logic in its action, it certainly escapes
the ability of humans to comprehend (as the mental power
of humans to imagine a 'before the universe' condition
goes, the 'big bang' does not appear more comprehensible
than the six-day creation). And so the 'cosmic fear' is also
the horror of the unknown: the terror of *uncertainty*.

It is also a deeper terror – of helplessness, to which
uncertainty is but a contributing factor. Helplessness becomes salient once the laughably brief mortal life is meas-
ured against the *eternity* – and the minute plot occupied by
humankind against the *infinity* – of the universe. *The
sacred, we may say, is a reflection of that experience of helplessness.* The sacred is what transcends our powers of compre-
hension, communication, action.

Bakhtin suggests that cosmic fear is used (reprocessed,
recycled) by all religious systems. The image of God,
the supreme ruler of the universe and its inhabitants,
is moulded out of the familiar emotion of fear of vulnerability and trembling in the face of impenetrable and irrep-
arable uncertainty.[28] Leszek Kołakowski explains religion
by human belief in the insufficiency of humans own
resources.

The modern mind was not necessarily atheistic. War
against God, the frantic search for proof that 'God does
not exist' or 'died', was left to the radical margins. What
the modern mind did, however, was to make God irrelevant to human business on earth. Modern science
emerged when a language had been constructed that

allowed whatever was learned about the world to be nar-
rated in non-teleological terms, that is with no reference to
'purpose' or divine intention. 'If God's mind is inscrutable, let us stop wasting time on reading the unreadable
and concentrate on what we, humans, can understand and
do.' Such a strategy led to spectacular triumphs of science
and its technological arm. But it also had far-reaching, and
not necessarily benign and beneficial, consequences for
the modality of human-being-in-the-world. The authority
of the sacred, and more generally our concern with eternity
and eternal values, were its first and most prominent
casualties.

The modern strategy consists in slicing the great issues
that transcend human power into smaller tasks which
humans can handle (for instance, the replacement of the
hopeless fight against *inevitable* death with the effective
treatment of many avoidable and curable diseases). The
'big issues' are not resolved but suspended, pushed aside,
removed from the agenda; not so much forgotten as
seldom recalled. Worry about the 'now' leaves no room
for the eternal and no time to reflect on it. In a fluid,
constantly changing environment the idea of eternity, perpetual duration or lasting value immune to the flow of time
has no grounding in human experience.

The speed of change delivers a death blow to the value
of durability: 'old' or 'long-lasting' becomes a synonym of
the old-fashioned, the outdated, something that has 'out-
lived its usefulness' and so is destined shortly to end up on
the rubbish heap.

When compared to the lifespan of the objects serving
human life and the institutions framing it, and to the style
of life itself, individual (bodily) human existence appears
to have the longest life expectancy; in fact, to be *the only*
entity with a rising, rather than fast shrinking, life expectancy. There are fewer and fewer things around – apart

from those that are cut out from the flow of daily life and mummified for leisure-time tourist enjoyment – that have seen times preceding the individual's birth; and even fewer that, having come on the scene later, can be reasonably expected to outlive their spectators.

The rule of the 'delay of gratification' no longer seems sensible advice as it still did in Max Weber's time. The worries recorded by Pascal have taken a different and unexpected turn: whoever may be concerned these days with longer-lasting things, let them better invest in the prolongation of individual bodily life than in 'eternal causes'. Marching in the advance units of the liquid modern army, we can no longer understand suicide bombers who sacrifice their earthly life, with all the pleasures it might hold in store, for an everlasting cause or eternal bliss. Given their evident frailty and transience, all things other than individual survival seem a poor investment. Their sole sensible use is to serve the individual's survival. Their potential gratification and delight is better savoured and consumed right now, on the spot, before it starts fading, as it surely soon will.

This is arguably the greatest challenge 'the sacred' has faced in its long history. Not that we now deem ourselves self-sufficient and omnipotent and no longer feel inadequate, helpless, insufficiently resourceful (we have not got rid of the feelings which Kołakowski pinpointed as the source of religious sentiments). It is rather that we have been trained to stop worrying about things which apparently stay stubbornly beyond our power (and so also about things stretching beyond our lifespan) and to concentrate our attention and energy instead on the tasks within our (individual) reach, competence and capacity for consumption. We are diligent and intelligent trainees; and so we demand that in order to earn our concern, things and issues must explain why they deserve our attention.

And this they can do through convincing proof of their use. The delay of gratification being no longer a sensible option, both delivery and use, as well as the gratification the goods promise, must in addition be instantaneous. Things must be ready for consumption on the spot; tasks must bring results before attention drifts to other endeavours; issues must bear fruits before the cultivating zeal runs out. Immortality? Eternity? Fine – where is the theme park where I can experience them, on the spot?

We have landed in a fully and truly foreign country ... An unknown, unexplored, unmapped land – we have not been here before, we have not heard of it before. All cultures we know of, at all times, tried, with mixed success, to bridge the gap between the brevity of mortal life and the eternity of the universe. Each culture offered a formula for the alchemist's feat: a reforging of base, fragile and transient substances into precious metals which would resist erosion, be everlasting. We are perhaps the first generation to enter life and live it without such a formula.

Christianity imbued the laughably short sojourn on earth with the tremendous significance of being the only chance to decide the quality of eternal spiritual existence. Baudelaire saw the artist's mission as unpacking the immortal kernel out of the shell of the fleeting moment. From Seneca to Durkheim, sages kept reminding everyone keen to listen that true happiness (unlike momentary and elusive pleasures) could be attained only in association with things that would last longer than the bodily life of a human being. To an average contemporary reader, such suggestions are incomprehensible and sound redundant. Bridges connecting mortal life to eternity, laboriously built over millennia, are cast out of use.

We have not been in a world deprived of such bridges before. It is too early to say what we may find, or what condition we may find ourselves in, living in such a land.

*The philosopher of Slovenian origin Slavoj Žižek has written passionate
pages against the so-called Western identity. But we have to bitterly observe
that the present international tensions are being explained with the thesis of
the clash of civilizations. It seems that all the different meanings which are
attached to the use of the term 'identity' contribute to an undermining of
the bases of universalistic thought, careful as it is to maintain that fragile
balance between individual rights and collective rights. A real paradox, don't
you think?*

Yes, 'identity' is a hopelessly ambiguous idea and a
double-edged sword. It may be a war-cry of individuals,
or of the communities that wish to be imagined by them.
At one time the edge of identity is turned against 'collective pressures' by individuals who resent conformity and
hold dear their own beliefs (which 'the group' would decry
as prejudices) and their own ways of living (which 'the
group' would condemn as cases of 'deviation' or 'silliness',
but at any rate of abnormality, needing to be cured or
punished). At another time it is the group that turns the
edge against a larger group that is accused of a wish to
devour or destroy it, of a vicious and ignoble intention to
smother a smaller group's difference, to force it or induce
it to surrender its own 'collective self', lose face, dissolve
. . . In both cases, though, 'identity' appears to be a war-cry
used in a *defensive* war: an individual against the assault of
a group, a smaller and weaker (and for this reason
threatened) group against a bigger and more resourceful
(and for that reason threatening) totality.

The sword of identity happens, however, also to be
wielded by the other – bigger and stronger – side. That
side wishes to play down the differences, wishes the presence of differences to be accepted as inevitable and lasting,
while insisting that they are not important enough to pre-
vent allegiance to a larger totality which is ready to embrace and provide a home for all those differences and
their carriers.

You could see the sword of identity brandished by both sides and cutting both ways in the times of 'nation-building': wielded in defence of smaller, local languages, memories, customs and habits against 'those in the capital' who promoted homogeneity and demanded uniformity – as well as in the 'cultural crusade' waged by the advocates of national unity who aimed to extirpate the 'provinciality', parochialism, *esprit de clocher* of local communities or ethnicities. National patriotism itself deployed its troops on two frontlines: against 'local particularism', in the name of a shared national fate and interests; and against 'rootless cosmopolitanism' that viewed and treated the nationalists in just the way the nationalists viewed and treated the 'narrow-minded provincial bumpkins' because of their loyalty to ethnic, linguistic or cultic idiosyncrasies.

Identity, let us be clear about it, is a 'hotly contested concept'. Whenever you hear that word, you can be sure that there is a battle going on. A battlefield is identity's natural home. Identity comes to life only in the tumult of battle; it falls asleep and silent the moment the noise of the battle dies down. Cutting both ways cannot therefore be avoided. It can perhaps be *wished* away (and commonly is, by philosophers striving for logical elegance), but it cannot be *thought* away, and even less can it be *done* away with in human practice. 'Identity' is a simultaneous struggle against dissolution and fragmentation; an intention to devour and at the same time a stout refusal to be eaten ...

At least in their pure and explicitly admitted essence, liberalism and communitarianism are two opposite attempts to reforge the sword of identity into a single-edged sabre. They mark the imaginary poles of a continuum along which all real identity battles are fought and all identity practices are plotted. Each one of them exploits in full only one of the two values similarly cherished and equally indispensable for the sake of a decent, fully fledged human existence: *freedom* of choice, and the *security* offered by belonging. And each does it, explicitly or implicitly, by upgrading one of the two values and down-grading the other. But 'really waged identity battles' and 'really performed identity practices' come nowhere near the purity of theories and declared political platforms. They are, and cannot but be, compounds of the 'liberal' demands for the freedom to self-define and self-assert, on the one hand, and the 'communitarian' appeals to a 'total-ity greater than the sum of its parts' as well as to its priority over each part's disruptive drives, on the other.

The two postulates sit awkwardly together. Their com-pany seems to 'make sense' when stated in the concrete terms of specific (genuine or putative) conflicts – 'You need to surrender your personal interests for the sake of the solidarity which your group needs to resist an even larger group that intends to take away whatever you hold dear and violate your interests. United we stand, divided we fall' – but not if expressed in terms of universal principles that are and will stay incompatible. In the practice of identity wars, both communitarian and liberal principles are enlisted and deployed in the battlefield next to each other. Distilled from the hot messiness of the battlefield and subjected to the judgement of cool reason, however, they immediately re-state their opposition. Life is richer, and less elegant, than any of the principles intended to guide it . . .

This does not mean, though, that philosophers will ever stop trying to straighten up the twisted and reconcile the incompatible. (A recent example is Will Kymlicka's at-tempt to argue the case away from the confusion of the battlefield and not just into a temporary armistice, but into an essential affinity and permanent alliance between benign liberal tenets and harsh communitarian demands. It is tempting to take Kymlicka's reasoning *ad absurdum* and to suggest that what he proposes in the last resort is that the duty to accept the group's pressure and to surrender to its demands is an indispensable part of the liberal's 'individual rights' bill.) However ingenious and logically elegant, philosophical efforts to argue the genuine contradiction out of existence would hardly have much impact on the current identity wars (apart from offering absolution and a blessing). They may, however, exert a rather adverse influence on our clarity of vision and our understanding of what we see. They steer dangerously close to George Orwell's 'newspeak'.

I guess that all such considerations confirm your suspicion that 'different meanings attached to the use of the term "identity" undermine the bases of universalistic thought'. Identity battles cannot do their job of identification without dividing as much as, or more than, they unite. Their inclusive intentions mingle with (or rather are complemented by) intentions to segregate, exempt and exclude.

There is but one exception to that rule – Kant's *allgemeine Vereinigung der Menschheit*, the truly, completely inclusive identity of the human race – which in his view was exactly what Nature, having put us on a spherical planet, must have intended our shared future to be. In our current practice, however, 'humanity' is just one of the innumerable identities currently engaged in a war of mutual attrition. Regardless of the truth or untruth of Kant's supposition that the unity of humankind has been predesigned as the outcome of that war, 'humanity' does not seem to enjoy any evident advantage in weapons or strategy in comparison with other fighters that are smaller in size but apparently more versatile and resourceful. Like other postulated identities, the ideal of 'humanity' as an identity embracing all other identities can ultimately rely solely on the dedication of its postulated adherents.

Alongside its less inclusive competitors, 'humanity' so far looks handicapped and weaker, rather than privileged and stronger. Unlike many other competing identities, it lacks coercive arms – political institutions, legal codes, courts of law, police – that could give courage to the meek, determination to the hesitating, and solidity to the achievements of proselytizing missions. As we have seen before, the planetary 'space of flows' is a 'politics free and ethics free area'. Every available anchorage for politics, law and ethical principles is so far under the administration of less inclusive, partial and divisive identities.

However hard we try to stretch our imagination, humanity's struggle for self-assertion does not seem easy, let alone a foregone conclusion. Its task is not just to repeat once more a feat performed many times before in the long history of humankind: to replace one, narrower identity by another that is more inclusive, and to push back the boundary of exclusion. The kind of challenge faced by the ideal of 'humanity' has not been confronted before, because an 'all-inclusive community' was never put on the agenda. This challenge is to be faced up to today by a fragmented, deeply divided human species, armed with no weapons except the enthusiasm and dedication of its militants.

Nonetheless, there is a nation which has been trying to institutionalize the co-presence of collective, but specific, identities and, in doing so, it has almost ended up relegating the universalistic character of modern law to a few norms only. Of course, I'm referring to the US. But even in this case, we must observe that the bringing into question of a mutable institutional frame based on the recognition of partial identities has been carried out in the name of ancestral identities. What, in the melting pot, did not work?

Again your observations are spot on. The two things go together – the thinness of the set of beliefs, symbols and rules that bind all polity members, and the richness, density and diversity of alternative (ethnic, historic, religious, sexual, linguistic, etc.) tokens of identity. There are other examples similar to the US (even if the 'melting pot' is a specifically American invention and dream). The situation is quite similar in other 'settlers' lands' (Australia, Canada), where the immigrants found no dominant and uncontested, historically formed culture that could serve as a pattern of adaptation and assimilation for every other newcomer, demanding universal obedience and getting it. Quite a few immigrants chose their new country hoping on the contrary to retain, develop and practise undisturbed their religious or ethnic distinctions that were under threat in their countries of origin. In the US, Australia or Canada the sole thing required from the incomers was to swear allegiance to the laws of the country (something like Habermas's 'constitutional patriotism') – otherwise, complete freedom was promised (and granted) in all matters where the constitution was silent.

What was made obligatory as a condition of citizenship had too little content to suffice for a full-blooded identity, and so to an extent greater than elsewhere the task of constructing a complete identity became a 'do-it-yourself' job. And it was undertaken and practised as such. America is a land not only of many ethnicities and religious denominations, but also of widespread, continuous, obsessive experimentation with all sorts of 'raw materials' that can be used in shaping up an identity. Virtually any material has been tried, whatever has not been tried will be – and the consumer market rejoices, filling warehouses and shop shelves with ever new, original, tempting because as yet untasted and untested, tokens of identity. There is also another phenomenon to note: the rapidly shrinking life expectation of most assumed identities coupled with the fast growing speed of their turnover. Individual biographies are all too often stories of discarded identities...

If we judge the results of all that by the American case, such a response to identity problems did not prove to be an unmitigated blessing. With the political state programmatically neutral and indifferent to the 'cottage industry' of identities, and abstaining from passing a judgement on the relative values of cultural choices and from promoting a shared model of togetherness, there are few if any shared values to hold society together. 'Our American way of life' to which American politicians constantly refer boils down in the last resort to the absence of any agreed and universally practised 'way of life' apart from the consent, willing or reluctant, to leave the selection of a 'way of life' to private initiative and to the resources at the disposal of individual citizens. When it comes to cultural preferences and choices, there is perhaps more disruption and antagonism than unity; conflicts are numerous and tend to be bitter and violent. This is a constant threat to social integration – and also to the feeling of individual security and self-assurance. This in turn creates and maintains a state of high anxiety. As an individual business conducted with few (and constantly changing) orientation points, the task of putting one's self-identity together, of making it coherent and presenting it for public approval, requires lifelong attention, continuous vigilance, a huge and growing volume of resources and incessant effort with no hope of respite. Acute anxiety results and seeks outlets: its surplus needs to be unloaded. Hence the tendency to seek substitute 'supports for unity' – shared enemies on which may be unleashed the accumulating anger, moral panics and bouts of collective paranoia. There is a constant demand for public enemies ('reds under the beds', the 'underclass', or just 'those who hate us' or 'who hate our American way of life') against whom the otherwise scattered individuals, jealous of their privacy and mutually suspicious, can unite in a daily spectacle of Orwell's 'five minutes of hatred'. Patriotism in the 'constitutional' form may become, it seems, a violent affair, full of sound and fury. Loyalty to the law of the country cries out to be supplemented by shared hatred or shared fears.

In order to continue the discussion on the melting pot, I would like to suggest for you a topic which implies ambivalent answers. I'm referring to the criticism that some feminist scholars and philosophers have applied to the concept of identity. Even in this case we could say, paraphrasing Jean-Paul Sartre, that being born as women is not enough to make us women. It seems to me that this is present in some recent contributions coming from feminist theory; that is, the fact that identity is not seen as an unchangeable fact, but rather as something in progress, as a process. A good way out from the cage of identity: don't you agree?

The provisional nature of all and any identity and of all and any choice between the infinite multitude of cultural models on offer is not a discovery of feminists and even less their invention.

The idea that nothing in the human condition is given once and for all and is imposed with no right of appeal or reform – that everything that is needs to be 'made' first and once made can be changed endlessly – accompanied the modern era from its beginning; indeed, obsessive and compulsive change (variously called 'modernizing', 'progress', 'improvement', 'development', 'updating') is the hard core of the modern mode of being. You cease to be 'modern' once you stop 'modernizing', once you put your hands down and stop tinkering with what you are and what the world around you is.

Modern history was also (and still is) a continuous effort to push out further the limits of what can be changed at will by humans and 'improved' to better suit human needs or desires. It was also a relentless search for tools and the know-how that would permit the ultimate limits to be cancelled and abolished altogether. We have arrived as far as the hope of manipulating the genetic composition of human beings, which until recently was the very paragon of immutability, of the 'nature' that humans must obey. It would be strange indeed if even the allegedly most stubborn facets of identity, like the size and shape of the body or its sex, remained for long an exception resistant to that all-embracing modern tendency.

It took a few centuries to lift the dreams of Pico della Mirandola (of human beings becoming like the legendary Proteus, who changed his shape from one moment to another and drew freely whatever he might fancy at that moment from the bottomless container of possibilities) to the level of a universal creed. The freedom to change any aspect and trapping of individual identity is something most people deem today to be attainable right away, or at least they view it as a realistic prospect for the near future.

Selecting the means required to achieve an alternative identity of your choice is no longer a problem (if you have enough money, that is, to purchase its obligatory paraphernalia). There is some gear waiting for you in the shops that will transform you in no time into the character you want to be, want to be seen being and want to be recognized as being. To give you just one, most recent example: after the introduction of 'congestion charges' for car drivers in central London, being a 'scooter rider' has immediately become obligatory for fashion-minded Londoners (though, obviously, not for long...). It is not just the scooter that has become 'a must', but also the specially designed gear indispensable for everyone wishing to parade in public their new 'scooter-rider identity' – like a Dolce & Gabbana leather jacket, Adidas red high-top trainers, a Gucci silver helmet, or Jill Sander yellow wrap-around sunglasses...

On the other hand, the real problem and today's most common worry is the opposite quandary: which one of the alternative identities to select and how long to hold on to it once the choice has been made? If in the past the 'art of life' consisted mostly in finding the right means to a given end, it is now a question of trying, one after another, all the (infinitely many) ends which can be obtained with the help of the means already possessed or within reach. Identity building has taken the form of unstoppable experimentation. Experiments never end. You try one identity at a time, but so many others, as yet untried, wait round the corner for you to pick them up. Many more undreamt-of identities are still to be invented and coveted in your lifetime. You'll never know for sure whether the identity you are currently parading is the best you can get and the one most likely to give you the most satisfaction.

Your bodily sexual equipment is just one of those resources at your disposal that, like all other resources, can be used for all sorts of purposes and put into the service of a whole range of objectives. The challenge, it seems, is to stretch the pleasure-generating potential of that 'natural equipment' to the utmost – by trying one by one all known kinds of 'sexual identity', and perhaps inventing still more on the way.

One of the most disquieting phenomena we have been witnessing is religious fundamentalism. Beyond the theological disputes that have accompanied the spreading of these movements, their essentially political character seems to me self-evident, be they in India, or in the Arab world, or the Moral Majority in the US. This phenomenon has been licking even the coasts of the state of Israel. What do you think of religious fundamentalism?

All three major religions – Christianity, Islam, Judaism – have their fundamentalisms. And we may guess that contemporary religious fundamentalism is a combined effect of two partly related, partly separate developments.

One is the erosion, and a threat of yet more erosion, of the 'hard core', the solid canon that held together the congregation of the faithful. That canon is increasingly frayed and blurred at the fringes and undoing, even falling apart, at its seams. Sects, which the churches view with apprehension as arguably the greatest threat to their unity, multiply – and the churches are manoeuvred into the position of besieged fortresses and/or 'permanent counter-reformation'. The canon of faith needs to be defended tooth and nail and restated daily, absentmindedness is suicidal, vigilance is the order of the day, the 'fifth column' (anything lukewarm and vacillating inside the congrega-tion) must be spotted in time and nipped in the bud.

Another development can perhaps be traced to the same roots (namely to the new liquid form our modern life has taken), but it primarily concerns the involuntary/compul-sive choosers we have all become in our deregulated, frag-mented, underdefined, underdetermined, unpredictable, out-of-joint and largely uncontrollable social setting. I have already stressed a number of times that, with all its coveted advantages, the life condition of a chooser-by-necessity is also an utterly unnerving experience. A chooser's life is an insecure life. The value conspicuously missing is that of confidence and trust and so also of self-assurance. Funda-mentalism (also religious fundamentalism) offers that value. By invalidating in advance all competing propos-itions and refusing a dialogue and argument with dissenters and 'heretics', it instils a feeling of certainty and sweeps away all doubt from the simple, easy to absorb code of behaviour it offers. It hands over the comforting sense of security to be gained and savoured inside the tall and im-penetrable walls which cut off the chaos reigning outside.

Certain varieties of fundamentalist churches are particu-larly attractive to the deprived and impoverished part of the population, those who are stripped of human dignity and humiliated – people who can do little more than watch with a mixture of envy and resentment the consumer revelry and

light-hearted ways of the better off (black Muslims in the
US, and Sephardic immigrants gathering in the oriental
synagogue in an Ashenazi-ruled Israel are spectacular,
though by no means the only, examples). To such people,
fundamentalist congregations provide a tempting and welcome shelter unavailable elsewhere. These congregations
pick up the tasks and duties abandoned by the retreating
social state. They also offer the most painfully missing
ingredient of a decent human life, refused to them by society at large: a sense of purpose, of meaningful life (or
meaningful death), of a rightful and dignified place in the
overall scheme of things. They also promise to defend their
faithful against the enforced, stereotyping and stigmatizing
'identities' imposed by the forces that rule the hostile and
inhospitable 'world out there' – or even turn the accusations
against the accusers, proclaiming that 'black is beautiful'
and thus recasting the alleged liabilities as assets.

Fundamentalism (including religious fundamentalism)
is not just a religious phenomenon. It draws its strength
from many sources. To be fully understood, it must be
seen against a background of the new global inequality and
the untamed injustice reigning in the global space.

*During the last years, we have witnessed the growth of a very differentiated
social movement which is against the neoliberalist globalization. A movement
which often speaks the languages of local identities, threatened by economic
development. Nonetheless I feel that, in this very same movement, there seems
to be a strong ambivalence. Identity can be a path towards emancipation, but it
can also be a form of oppression. What do you think of it?*

It is of course too early to pass final judgement on the
historical significance of the so-called 'anti-globalist'
movements. I think, by the way, that the term is misleading. One cannot be 'against globalization' as one cannot be
against the Sun's eclipse; the problem, and the movement's

proper issue, is not how to 'undo' the unification of the
planet, but how to tame and control the heretofore wild
globalization processes – and how to turn them from a
threat into a chance for humanity.

One thing, however, seems to be clear: 'think globally, act
locally' is a misconceived and even harmful slogan. There
are no local solutions to globally generated troubles. Global
problems can only be resolved, if at all, by global actions.
Seeking salvage from the pernicious effects of untamed and
uncontrolled globalization by withdrawing into a cosy
neighbourhood, locking the gates and shutting the windows
only helps to perpetuate the 'Wild West', 'frontierland' conditions of lawlessness, of 'catch-as-catch-can' strategies, of
rampant inequality and universal vulnerability. Untamed
and destructive global forces thrive on the fragmentation
of the political stage and the splitting of potentially global
politics into a collection of endlessly quarrelling local ego-
isms bargaining for a larger share of the crumbs falling from
the festive table of the global robber barons. Anyone advo-
cating 'local identities' as an antidote against the misdeeds
of the globalizers plays their game – and into their hands.

Globalization has now reached the point of no return. We
are all dependent on each other, and the only choice we
have is between mutually assuring each other's vulnerability and mutually assuring our shared security. Bluntly: to
swim together or to sink together. I believe that for the first
time in human history everybody's self-interest and ethical
principles of mutual respect and care point in the same
direction and demand the same strategy. From a curse,
globalization may yet turn into a blessing: 'humanity'
never had a better chance! Whether this happens, whether
the chance is indeed taken before it is lost, remains however
an open question. The answer depends on us.

We do not live at the end of history, or even at a beginning of the end. We are at the threshold of another great

transformation: the global forces let loose, and their blind and hurtful effects, have to be put under popular democratic control and forced to respect and observe the ethical principles of human cohabitation and social justice. What institutional forms that transformation will produce it is far too early to surmise: history cannot be pre-empted. What we can be reasonably sure of is, however, that the test such forms will have to pass to fulfil their intended role will be the raising of our identities to the planetary level – the level of humanity.

Sooner or later we will have to draw conclusions from our irreversible mutual dependency. Unless we do that, all the gains that the high and mighty enjoy under conditions of global disorder (resenting and resisting for that reason every attempt to establish planetary institutions of democratic control, law and justice) will go on being gained at enormous costs to the quality of life and dignity of great numbers of human beings, and will add further to the already formidable insecurity and frailty of the world we all jointly inhabit.

One of the means, one of the instruments for playing with identity is the internet. In fact, on the World Wide Web we can communicate creating fake identities. Don't you think that the issue of identity, exactly in cyberspace, disintegrates until it is only a pastime?

In our fluid world, committing oneself to a single identity for life, or even for less than a whole life but for a very long time to come, is a risky business. Identities are for wearing and showing, not for storing and keeping. That much already follows from what we have been talking about so far. But if this is the condition under which we all have to go about our daily business, willy-nilly, it would be unwise to blame electronic devices, like internet chat groups or mobile telephone 'networks', for this state of affairs. It is rather the other way round: it is because we are endlessly forced to twist and mould our identities, and are not allowed to stick to one identity even if we want to, that electronic instruments to do just that come in handy and tend to be enthusiastically embraced by millions.

You say 'fake identities' . . . but you can say that only if you assume that there is such a thing as a one and only 'true identity'. This assumption, however, does not appear credible to people running after changing fashions – always just *fashions*, but always *obligatory* as long as they remain in fashion . . . This is how Henrik Ibsen's hero Peer Gynt, obsessed all his life with finding his 'true identity', summed up his life strategy: 'I tried to make time stand still – by dancing!'

Peer Gynt, the play published in 1867, ought to be read and reflected upon these days by everyone baffled and disturbed by the elusiveness of identity – and this means, indeed, everybody. All present-day troubles are, prophetically, foreseen and explored there.

What Peer Gynt was afraid of more than of anything else was 'to know that you can't ever free yourself', and 'to be stuck' in one identity 'for the rest of your days'.[29] 'This thing of having no line of retreat . . . That's a condition I'll never give in to.' Why was such a prospect terrifying? Because 'who knows what's round the corner'; what seems beautiful and comfortable and dignified now may turn out to be, once round the corner, ugly, unfit and base. To escape such an unenviable eventuality, Peer Gynt decided on what can only be called 'pre-emptive strikes': 'The whole art of taking risks, / of having the strength of mind to act, / is this: to keep your freedom of choice', 'to know that other days will come', 'to know that behind you there is always / a bridge, if you have to beat a retreat'. To make such a strategy bear fruit, Peer Gynt resolved (mistakenly, as it transpired at the end of the story) 'to sever the ties that are holding you / on every side to home and friends – / blow all your worldly goods sky-high – / bid a fond farewell to the pleasures of love'. Even being an emperor of a kingdom is too risky a business, burdened with too many obligations and constraints. Gynt wished to be only 'the Emperor of Human Experience'. He followed that strategy throughout – only to wonder at the end of his long life, puzzled, sad and confused, 'where Peer Gynt has been all these years? . . . Where was I myself, the entire, true man?' Only Solveig, the great love of his youth who stayed faithful to her love when the lover resolved to become the Emperor of Human Experience, could answer that question – and she did. Where were you? 'In my faith, in my hope, and in my love.'

We are today, a century and a half later, consumers in a consumers' society. Consumer society is market society; we are all *in* and *on* the market, simultaneously customers and commodities. No wonder that the use/consumption of human relations and so, by proxy, also our identities (we identify ourselves by reference to people to whom we are related) catches up, and fast, with the pattern of car use/consumption, imitating the cycle that starts from purchase and ends with waste disposal.

A growing number of observers reasonably expect friends and friendships to play a vital role in our thoroughly individualized society. With the structures of the traditional supports of social cohesion fast falling apart, relations woven out of friendship could become our life-jackets or lifeboats. Ray Pahl, pointing out that in our times of choice friendship, 'the archetypal social relationship of choice', is our natural choice, calls friendship the 'social convoy' of late modern life.[30] Reality seems to be somewhat less straightforward, however. In this 'late modern' or liquid modern life, relationships are an ambiguous matter and tend to be the focus of a most acute and nerve-wracking ambivalence: the price for the companionship which all of us ardently desire is invariably a, partial at least, surrender of independence, however dearly one would wish the first without the second . . .

Continuous ambivalence results in cognitive dissonance, a state of mind notoriously demeaning, incapacitating and difficult to endure. It invites in turn the usual repertory of mitigating stratagems, among which the marking down, playing down and belittling of one of the two irreconcilable values is the most commonly resorted to. Subjected to contradictory pressures, many a relationship, meant anyway to be only 'until further notice', will snap. Snapping is a reasonable expectation, something to think about in advance and be prepared to face.

When the high likelihood of waste is calculated in the process of tying up relationship bonds, foresight and prudence advise taking care of the waste-disposal facility well in advance. After all, sober-minded urban developers (in the US, at least) would not risk starting on a building unless a demolition permit was obtained; generals are loath to send their troops into battle before a credible exit scenario is scripted; and employers all around complain that it is the assumption of their employees' earned rights and the constraints imposed on firing them that makes the extension of employment all but impossible.

Partnerships instantly entered, fast consumed and disposed of on demand have their unpleasant side-effects. The spectre of the rubbish heap is never far away. After all, speed and waste-disposal services are available to both sides. You may end up in a plight like the one described by Oliver James: poisoned with 'a constant sense of the lack of others in your life, with feelings of emptiness and loneliness akin to bereavement'.[31] You may be 'forever fearful you will be dropped by lovers and friends'.

What we all seem to fear, whether we are suffering from 'dependent depression' or not, whether we are in the full light of day or harassed by nocturnal hallucinations, is abandonment, exclusion, being rejected, blackballed, disowned, dropped, stripped of what we are, not allowed to be what we wish to be. We fear being left alone, helpless and hapless. We fear being denied company, loving hearts, helping hands. We fear being dumped in the scrapyard. What we miss most is the certainty that all that won't happen – not to us. We miss exemption from the universal and ubiquitous threat of exemption . . .

The horrors of exclusion emanate from two sources, though we are seldom clear about their nature, let alone strive to tell one from the other.

There are the seemingly random, haphazard and utterly unpredictable shifts and drifts of what for the lack of a more precise name are called 'forces of globalization'. They change beyond recognition, and without warning, the familiar land-scapes and cityscapes where the anchors of our durable and reliable security used to be cast. They reshuffle people and play havoc with their social identities. They may transform us, from one day to another, into homeless vagabonds with no fixed address or identity. They may withdraw our certificates of identity or invalidate the identities certified. And they remind us daily that they can do it with impunity – when they dump on our doorsteps those people who have already been rejected, forced to run for their lives or to scramble away from home for the means to stay alive, robbed of their identities and self-esteem. We talk these days of nothing with greater solemnity or more relish than of 'networks' of 'connection' or 'relationships', only because the 'real stuff' – the closely knit networks, firm and secure connections, fully fledged relationships – have all but fallen apart.

I needed this longish diversion to confront your question: to explain that if we talk compulsively about networks and try obsessively to conjure them (or at least their phantoms) out of 'speed dating' and magic incantations of mobile telephone 'messaging', it is because we painfully miss the safety nets which the true networks of kinship, friends and brothers-in-fate used to provide matter-of-factly, with or without our efforts. Mobile-telephone directories stand for the missing community and the hope is that they will deputize for the missing intimacy; they are expected to carry a load of expectations they lack the strength to lift, let alone to hold.

Andy Hargreaves, let me quote him once more, writes on 'episodic strings of tiny interactions' that are increasingly replacing 'sustained family conversations and relationships'.[32] Exposed to the 'contacts made easy' by electronic technology, we lose the ability to enter into spontaneous interaction with real people. In fact, we grow shy of face-to-face contacts. We tend to reach for our mobiles and furiously press buttons and knead messages in order to avoid making ourselves hostage to fate – in order to escape from complex, messy, unpredictable, difficult to interrupt and to opt out from interactions with those 'real people' physically present around us. The wider (even if shallower) our phantom communities, the more daunting appears the task of sewing together and holding together real ones.

As always, consumer markets are all too eager to help us out of the predicament. Taking a hint from Stjepan Mestrovič,[33] Hargreaves suggests that 'emotions are extracted from this time-starved world of shrinking relationships and reinvested in consumable things. Advertising associates automobiles with passion and desire, and mobile telephones with inspiration and lust.' But however hard the merchants try, the hunger they promise to satiate won't go away. Human beings may have been recycled into consumables, but consumables cannot be made into humans. Not into the kinds of humans that inspire our desperate search for roots, kinship, friendship and love – not humans one could *identify with*.

It needs to be admitted that consumable substitutes have an edge over the 'real stuff'. They promise freedom from the chores of endless negotiation and uneasy compromise; they swear to put paid to the vexing need for self-sacrifice, concessions, meeting half-way that all intimate and loving bonds will sooner or later require. They come with an offer of recuperating your losses if you find all such strains too heavy to bear. Their sellers also vouch for an easy and frequent replacement of goods the moment you no longer find a use for them, or when other, new, improved and still more seductive goods appear in sight. In short, consumables embody the ultimate non-finality and revocability of choices and the ultimate disposability of the objects chosen. Even more importantly, they seem to put us in control. It is we, the consumers, who draw the line between the useful and the waste. Having consumables for partners, we can stop worrying about ending in the refuse bin. Or can we?

From my point of view, the last question about the internet asks for attention to the role of new media in the formation of public opinion and the collective identity. What do I have in mind? For me, the book needs to explore two other themes: identity and new media, and the 'policy of identity' (the crisis of multiculturalism).

We have discussed that convoluted issue, 'multiculturalism', before. I suggested then that what is meat for some may be poison for quite a few others. The proclamation of the 'multicultural age' reflects in my opinion the life experience of the new global elite which, whenever they travel (and they travel a lot, by plane or on the World Wide Web) find other members of the same global elite who speak the same language and worry about the same things. Lecturing around Europe and beyond, I have been struck by the fact that the questions I am asked by the audience are the same everywhere...

The proclamation of the multicultural age is, however, at the same time a declaration of intent: of a refusal to pass judgement and to take a stand; a declaration of indifference, of hands being washed of petty quarrels about preferred styles of life or favourite values. It displays the new 'cultural omnivorousness' of the global elite: let's treat the world as a gigantic department store with shelves full of the most varied offers, and let's be free to roam one floor after another, try and taste every item on display, pick them up to our heart's desire.

This is an attitude of people who travel – who travel even when they stay put in their homes or offices. This is not, however, an attitude easy to adopt for the great majority of the planet's residents, who stay fixed to the place of their birth and who, if they wished to go elsewhere in search of a better or simply a different life, would be stopped at the nearest border, confined in camps for 'illegal immigrants' or 'sent back home'. That majority is excluded from the planetary feast. No 'multicultural bazaar' for them. They often find themselves, as Maria Markus has suggested, in a state of 'suspended existence',[34] holding on to an image of a past that has been lost but is dreamt of being restored, and of the present as an aberration and the work of forces of evil. They 'close off' the bewildering cacophony of cultural messages.

At no point in the last two centuries or so have the languages spoken respectively by the educated and well-off elite and the rest of 'the people' differed from each other so strongly, and have the experiences spoken of in these languages been so different from each other.

From the advent of the modern state, the educated elite saw itself (rightly or wrongly, for better or worse) as the avant-garde, the advanced units of the nation: we are here to lead the rest of the people to where we have already arrived – others will follow us, and it is our task to make them move quickly. This sense of a collective mission has now been all but abandoned. 'Multiculturalism' is a gloss on that retreat (or an excuse for it). It is as if those who praise and applaud multicultural divisions were implying: we are free to become whatever we wish to be, but 'the people' would rather stick to what they were born into and groomed to remain. And let them – that is their business, not ours.

You ask about the role of the media in the production of current identities. I'd rather say that the media supply the raw stuff which their viewers use to tackle the ambivalence of their social placement. Most TV viewers are painfully aware that they have been barred entry to the planetary 'polycultural' festivities. They do not live, and cannot dream of living, in the extraterritorial global space in which the 'cosmopolitan' cultural elite resides. The media supply 'virtual extraterritoriality', 'substitute extra-territoriality', 'imagined extraterritoriality' to the multi-tude of people who are denied access to the real one.

The effect of 'virtual extraterritoriality' is achieved by synchronizing the shift of attention and its objects over the vast expanses of the globe. Millions and hundreds of mil-lions watch and admire the same film stars or pop celeb-rities, move simultaneously from 'heavy metal' to rap, from flared trousers to the last word in trainers, fulminate against the same (global) public enemy, fear the same (global) villain or applaud the same (global) saviour. For a time this lifts them spiritually above the ground from which they are not allowed to move physically.

Synchronization of focuses of attention and topics of conversation is not, of course, tantamount to a shared iden-tity, but the focuses and the topics drift on so rapidly that there is hardly time to grasp that truth. They tend to disap-pear from view and be forgotten before their bluff has had time to be called. But before they disappear they manage to alleviate the pain of exclusion. They create an illusion of freedom to choose such as Peer Gynt entertained and enjoyed, though living up to that illusion was a daunting task and an uphill struggle – spawning a lot of frustration and leaving behind little gain. The moments of happiness were interspersed with long periods of worry and sadness.

If you wish me to tie together the many threads which we started to spin but in most cases left hanging loose, I'd say that the ambivalence most of us experience most of the time when we are trying to answer the question of our identity is genuine. The confusion it causes in our minds is also genuine. There is no foolproof recipe for resolving the troubles to which that confusion leads, and there are no quick fixes or risk-free ways of dealing with all that. I'd say as well that despite all this we will have to confront the task of 'self-identification' over and over again and that the task has little chance of ever being brought to successful and permanently satisfactory completion. We are likely to be torn between the desire for an identity of our liking and choice, and the fear that once that identity has been acquired we may discover, as Peer Gynt did, that there is no 'bridge, if you have to beat a retreat'.

And beware of opting out from facing up to the challenge. Remember Stuart Hall's words:

> Since cultural diversity is, increasingly, the fate of the modern world, and ethnic absolutism a regressive feature of late-modernity, the greatest danger now arises from forms of national and cultural identity – new and old – which attempt to secure their identity by adopting closed versions of culture or community and by refusal to engage ... with the difficult problems that arise from trying to live with difference.[35]

Try, as much as you can, to steer clear of that danger.

Notes

1 See Siegfried Kracauer, *Ornament der Masse* (Suhrkamp, 1963).
2 'Une généalogie de l'insécurité contemporaine', interview with Philippe Robert, *Esprit* (Dec. 2002), pp. 35–58.
3 Giorgio Agamben, *Means without Ends*, trans. Vincenzo Binetti and Cesare Casarino (University of Minnesota Press, 2000), p. 21.
4 Jorge Luis Borges, 'Averroes' search', in *Collected Fictions*, trans. Andrew Hurley (Penguin, 1998), p. 241.
5 Jonathan Matthew Schwartz, *Pieces of Mosaic* (Intervention Press, Holjberg, 1996), p. 132.
6 Lars Dencik, 'Transformation of identities in rapidly changing societies', in *The Transformation of Modernity: Aspects of the Past, Present and Future of an Era*, ed. Mikael Carleheden and Michael Hviid Jacobsen (Ashgate, 2001), p. 194.
7 Clifford Stoll, *Silicon Snakeoil* (Doubleday, 1995), p. 58.
8 Charles Handy, *The Elephant and the Flea* (Hutchinson, 2001), p. 204.
9 Andy Hargreaves, *Teaching in the Knowledge Society: Education in the Age of Insecurity* (Open University Press, 2003), p. 25.
10 Quoted after Hanna Mamzer, *Tozsamosc w podrozy* (Poznan, 2002), p. 13.

11   Monika Kostera, *Postmodernizm w zarzadzaniu* (Warsaw, 1996), p. 204.

12   Richard Sennett, 'Flexibilité sur la ville', *Manière de Voir*, 66 (Nov. – Dec. 2002), pp. 59–62.

13   Peter Beilharz, 'The logic of polarization: exclusion and exploitation', MS.

14   Richard Rorty, *Achieving our Country* (Harvard University Press, 1998), pp. 79, 91.

15   Richard Rorty, *Philosophy and Social Hope* (Penguin Books, 1999), p. 203.

16   Hauke Brunkhorst, 'Global society as the crisis of democracy', in *The Transformation of Modernity*, p. 233.

17   Alain Peyrefitte, *La société de confiance* (Odile Jacob, 1998), pp. 515 ff.

18   Robert Musil, *Diaries 1899–1941*, trans. Philip Payne (Basic Books, 1998), p. 52.

19   Beata Frydryczak, *Swiat jako kolekcja* (The World as a Collection) (Humaniora, 2002), pp. 52–5.

20   Tom Nairn, 'Demonizing nationalism', *London Review of Books*, 23 Feb. 1993.

21   René Girard, *Le bouc émissaire* (1982), here quoted in Yvonne Freccero's translation, *The Scapegoat* (Johns Hopkins University Press, 1986), pp. 14, 16, 21.

22   Geneviève Zubrzycki, 'The classical opposition between civic and ethnic models of nationhood: ideology, empirical reality and social scientific analysis', *Polish Sociological Review*, 3 (2002), pp. 275–95.

23   Erich Fromm, *The Art of Loving* (Thorson, 1995), p. vii.

24   *Observer Magazine*, 15 Dec. 2002, p. 43.

25   Barbara Ellen, 'Breaking up may be hard, but there is no harm in men learning the etiquette', *Observer Magazine*, 5 Jan. 2003, p. 7.

26   See Mikhail Bakhtin, *Rabelais and his World* (MIT Press, 1968) (translation of the Russian publication of 1965). Also Ken Hirschkop's apt summary in 'Fear and Democracy: an essay on Bakhtin's theory of carnival', *Associations*, 1 (1997), pp. 209–34.

27 Blaise Pascal, *Pensées*, here quoted after A. J. Krailsheimer's translation (Penguin, 1966), p. 48.

28 Let me just note, without developing the topic, that vulnerability – uncertainty and helplessness – is also the quality of the human condition out of which the *official* fear is moulded: the fear of *human* power, of man-made and man-held power. Such 'official fear' is construed after the pattern of the inhuman power reflected by (or, rather, emanating from) 'cosmic fear'. Earthly powers must shape themselves in the likeness of God to rub off some of His awesome, fear-inspiring power onto their own shoulders. They struggle to make themselves the source of uncertainty and incomprehension ('Glasnost' as intended by Gorbachev would sound a death knell for more than just the communist dictatorship); they draw their might and authority from their subjects' vulnerability.

29 *Peer Gynt* here quoted in the translation by Chistopher Fry and Johan Fillinger (Oxford University Press, 1970).

30 See Ray Pahl, *On Friendship* (Polity, 2000).

31 See Oliver James, 'Constant craving', *Observer Magazine*, 19 Jan. 2003, p. 71.

32 Hargreaves, *Teaching in the Knowledge Society*, p. 25.

33 Stjepan Mestrovič, *Postemotional Society* (Sage, 1997).

34 Maria R. Markus, 'Cultural pluralism and the subversion of the "taken for granted" world', in *Race Critical Theories*, ed. Philomena Essed and David Theo Goldberg (Blackwell, 2002), p. 401.

35 Stuart Hall, 'Culture, community, nation', *Cultural Studies*, 3 (1993), pp. 349–63.

Index